The Unknown Rapture Scriptures

Jonathan Hale

ISBN 978-1-7322191-0-6 (Paperback)

Copyright © 2017 by Jonathan Hale
All rights reserved. No part of this publication may be reproduced, distributed, or transmitted in any form or by any means, including photocopying, recording, or other electronic or mechanical methods, without the prior written permission of the author, except in the case of brief quotations embodied in critical reviews and certain other non-commercial uses permitted by copyright law.

Unless Otherwise stated, Scripture quotations are from the ESV® Bible (The Holy Bible, English Standard Version®), copyright © 2001 by Crossway, a publishing ministry of Good News Publishers. Used by permission. All rights reserved.

Contents

Method of Interpretation 1

Five Important Rapture Details 8

Linking Our Rapture Defining Scriptures 17

Finding Our Rapture Details in Revelation 22

The Six Chapters of the Rapture 29

Purposing an Exact Rapture Location in Revelation 41

The Sign of the Son of Man 48

The Voice of the Archangel 63

The Trumpet Call 79

The Saints are "Caught Up" (Rapture) 97

Why the Rapture's Location has been Unknown 113

The Church of Revelation 127

1
Method of Interpretation

The rapture is often taught as the church's evacuation. It is unlikely anyone would use this exact terminology, but much of the teachings on the rapture imply exactly that. In these teachings the church is evacuated and largely removed from the story of the upcoming end time events. Once safely evacuated, God figuratively carpet bombs the earth over and over before Jesus finally returns to crush the evildoers who survive.

This description may be a little overdramatic, but is the rapture really the evacuation of the church before God spends years repeatedly punishing the world? We will see throughout this book that this view is not consistent with the Bible. The rapture is not portrayed as an evacuation but as a great victory. However, the knowledge of this victory and its details has been lost to the church through numerous misinterpretations of scripture. These misinterpretations have had the effect of almost completely blotting out the church from the prophetic end time events.

The problem with many of the current interpretations of the rapture is the lack of scripture given to back them up. Most other studies will quote fewer than five passages directly referencing the rapture. They will quote much more than five total, but I am referring to verses "directly" speaking of the rapture. These books focus more on opinions and less on finding details in scripture.

In contrast our book will quote numerous verses directly speaking of the rapture. We will show over twenty scriptures in the Old Testament alone which "directly" speak of the day of the rapture. This "whole Bible" interpretation of the rapture will be a major difference between this and other books on this subject.

You may be wondering how we could possibly find such a numerous amount of verses directly speaking of the day of the rapture. We will do this by using a method in which the Bible interprets itself. The easiest way to explain this method is to give an example. Let's say you wanted to understand what "fear God" means in the following verse.

Leviticus 25:17
17 You shall not wrong one another, but you shall fear your God, for I am the LORD your God.

To find the answer we could read numerous Bible commentaries or look up the Hebrew word translated "fear", and we could certainly find an abundance of information using these methods. However, we can get a much more certain interpretation using only the Bible. You can notice that even this verse gives us a clue to the definition. "You shall not wrong one another", is put in direct contrast to fearing God. Therefore, someone who fears God will not wrong others. This partial definition can be expanded by finding other verses that mention the fear of God. If you did a word search combining the phrases "fear God" and "fear the LORD" these are some of the verses you would find.

Proverbs 14:2
2 Whoever walks in uprightness fears the LORD, but he who is devious in his ways despises him.

METHOD OF INTERPRETATION

Proverbs 8:13
¹³ The fear of the LORD is hatred of evil. Pride and arrogance and the way of evil and perverted speech I hate.

Exodus 14:31
Israel saw the great power that the Lord used against the Egyptians, so the people feared the Lord, and they believed in the Lord and in his servant Moses.

    We have now read four verses which help us to define the fear of God. There are many more than just these four. By reading and studying all these together we can get a very accurate idea of what the phrase "fear God" means in the Bible without using any external sources. If you used other methods to get the answer you could certainly get many opinions, but you would not have the same certainty in the accuracy of the answer.

    One great thing about the method we just used is this confidence we get in its accuracy. Let's say someone reads a verse from the Bible mentioning "the fear of God" and tells us, "fearing God is what the ungodly do when they continue to sin and know they will eventually be punished." We have already read four verses which contradict this definition and we could easily bring it to ten. If we can read ten separate verses in the Bible that all say the same thing we will not be fooled when told one of those ten verses means something different. This is how our method gives us confidence in our interpretation.

    Our method of interpretation requires us to have a starting point just as Leviticus 25:17 was our starting point in our example on fearing God. We will need to have some verses we know are speaking of the rapture before we can find other verses like them. Fortunately, there are two sections of scripture which are widely believed to be speaking of the rapture. Here is the first.

THE UNKNOWN RAPTURE SCRIPTURES

1 Thessalonians 4:16-17
¹⁶ For the Lord himself will descend from heaven with a cry of command, with the voice of an archangel, and with the sound of the trumpet of God. And the dead in Christ will rise first. ¹⁷ Then we who are alive, who are left, will be <u>caught up</u> together with them in the clouds to meet the Lord in the air, and so we will always be with the Lord.

"Rapture" is not a word from the original language this verse was written, but the underlined words "caught up", in the verse above, is the phrase from which we get the word "rapture". Since this is the case, this verse, more than any other, is the definition of the rapture. Now let's examine the second verse we will use to define the rapture.

Matthew 24:30-31
³⁰ Then will appear in heaven the sign of the Son of Man, and then all the tribes of the earth will mourn, and they will see the Son of Man coming on the clouds of heaven with power and great glory. ³¹ And he will send out his angels with a loud trumpet call, and they will gather his elect from the four winds, from one end of heaven to the other.

These last two sections of scripture are the two locations we will use as our definition of the rapture. These will be referred to as our "rapture defining scriptures" for the rest of this book. Just as in our example, which studied the phrase "fear God", we will be finding many other verses related to these two in order to get a better understanding of the event as a whole.

You are probably wandering if this method will be effective in helping us understand rapture prophecy? You have seen that it works for a simple phrase, but does it also work for a more complex prophecy? I want to remove any doubt you may have as early as possible. In the table on the following page you can see six Old Testament prophecies this method can link to one of our rapture defining scriptures.

METHOD OF INTERPRETATION

The Rapture from Matthew
Matthew 24:29-31

	Symbol or Direct Quote to be Matched with Old Testament Scripture	Old Testament Scriptural Match
Verse 29	Sun/Moon/Stars Turned to Darkness	Joel 2:10-11
		Isaiah 13:9-13
	The Heavens Shaken	Joel 3:14-16
Verse 30	Jesus Appears in the Sky	Zechariah 9:14
Verse 31	Those Coming from the Four Winds/The Ends of the Heavens	Ezekiel 37:7-9
		Isaiah 13:4-5a

As you can see there are symbols or direct quotes within our rapture defining scriptures we can match with Old Testament prophecies. We do not yet know if these matches are legitimate of coincidental. However, we will examine all these verses throughout the course of our study to determine if any or all of these are unknown rapture scriptures.

Most of the rest of the book will use the method we described to simultaneously achieve two goals:
1. We will find the exact place in the book of Revelation where the rapture occurs.
2. We will find as many verses as possible which speak of the rapture.

THE UNKNOWN RAPTURE SCRIPTURES

As our first goal implies, we need to start by answering what you would think is a very basic question. The rapture is often taught independently from the scriptures of the book of Revelation. Even though this is the case, almost everyone acknowledges the rapture occurs somewhere within the events of that book. Through our study of Old Testament and New Testament prophecies we will be able to find the exact place in Revelation where the rapture occurs. As we accomplish this we will be unlocking numerous details relating to the event (our second goal).

We will use a seven-step process to accomplish these two goals. Here is that process.

1. **Listing Details from our Rapture Defining Scriptures.**
   We will list five details about the rapture from our rapture defining scriptures. These are details referring to events near the time of the rapture. Just as we did in our example study on "fear God", we will be able to search for other places these five occur together. We will easily find these together in Revelation in a later step.
2. **Linking Our Rapture Defining Scriptures Together**
   We will prove our two rapture defining scriptures are speaking of the same event using the five details we found in step 1.
3. **Finding Our Rapture Details in Revelation.**
   We will find the five rapture details of step 1 in the book of Revelation. We will see that all five rapture details occur within nine verses of each other in Revelation 16. However, we will not yet know the location of the rapture since we will still not see the event where the Lord descends from heaven.
4. **Proving the Day of the Rapture Stretches Through Multiple Chapters of Revelation.**
   We will show that Revelation 14-19 all occurs on the same day of the five rapture details we found in

METHOD OF INTERPRETATION

Revelation 16. This gives us a window to search for the location where the Lord descends from heaven, as stated in each of our rapture defining scriptures.
5. **Purposing an exact point in Revelation where the Lord descends from heaven.**
    We will purpose an exact location where the Lord will descend from heaven in our Revelation 14-19 window.
6. **Confirming we have found the raptures location in Revelation.**
    We will go into great detail proving our hypothesized point for the rapture in Revelation (found in step 5) is the same event as our two rapture defining scriptures. Through this examination we will get a huge amount of detail on how the rapture will occur.
7. **Why Isn't the Raptures Location in Revelation Known?**
    Finally, we will address a major misunderstanding, dealing with Matthew 24, which is the main reason scholars have had difficulty locating the rapture in Revelation.

If this seems overwhelming or confusing do not worry. We will strive to make this as simple as possible as we go along.

One final word before we begin. Like me, many of you may have read or heard many teachings on Revelation and always gone away disappointed. Much is usually promised and very little delivered. Let me tell you that the rapture is described in great detail in the Bible, and this time I do not believe you will be disappointed. This book will give a level of detail on the rapture which I have never found in other studies, and will present them in the exciting way the Bible means them to be presented.

2

Five Important Rapture Details

Reporters waited outside the house of Harold Camping on May 22, 2011. He had predicted that the rapture would occur on the previous day. He had convinced a wide audience his interpretation was true through his platform on "Family Radio" and through millions of dollars of advertising money he had received through donations.

Reuters reported that he came out of his house saying he was "flabbergasted" that the rapture had not occurred. The very next day he reported the rapture would actually occur on October 21, 2011. Obviously that prediction proved false as well. This false prediction proved disastrous for Camping, and many of his former followers now viewed him as a cult leader, as reported by "Religion Dispatches".

Camping got off easy compared to some of his followers. As with many such movements many of his followers gave large amounts of money they could not afford to help fund the message of the coming rapture. Many likely sold their houses, quit their jobs, or made other crazy decisions based on their false belief in this teaching.

FIVE IMPORTANT RAPTURE DETAILS

This story is far from unique. The rapture has been one of the most debated and misinterpreted topics in the entire Bible. Almost every year reports are heard claiming someone has found the exact date the rapture will occur. Every year these teachings prove to be false as the date passes without event.

These false teachers likely started with a desire to find the truth, but at some point they began using a bad method of interpretation. Usually this involves them using their own wisdom and problem-solving skills independent from scripture. For example, by giving an exact date for the rapture they are going against the following scripture.

Matthew 24:26
36 "But concerning that day and hour no one knows, not even the angels of heaven, nor the Son, but the Father only.

As you can see if anyone gives an exact date for the rapture they are giving their own interpretation and not the interpretation given by the Bible.

With this in mind, I will not interpret the rapture using some claimed divine revelation or a series of logical arguments, but will be careful to focus entirely on what has already been written in the Bible. In fact, if it had been practical, I would have set "x" scripture verses one after another and proclaimed, "This is the interpretation". With that said let's begin finding details about the rapture directly from scripture.

In our first step we will find five details associated with the rapture which we will be able to find in Revelation. We will find these details in our rapture defining scripture from Matthew, since the chapter this passage is taken from provides a more detailed look at the events surrounding the rapture than the version in 1 Thessalonians. These details will be found in Matthew 24:26-44. This section of scripture describes the events surrounding the rapture and includes our rapture defining scripture in verses thirty and thirty-one. Three of our five rapture details will come directly from these verses while the other two will come from combining these verses with other scriptures. The importance in finding these five details is that all five will later be shown to occur within nine verses of each other in Revelation. This will mean we know the general location of the rapture in the end times prophecies.

Finding Rapture Detail 1 and 2

Let's begin our investigation by reading the first section of Matthew 24:26-44.

Matthew 24:26-31
^{26} So, if they say to you, 'Look, he is in the wilderness,' do not go out. If they say, 'Look, he is in the inner rooms,' do not believe it. ^{27} For as the lightning comes from the east and shines as far as the west, so will be the coming of the Son of Man. ^{28} Wherever the corpse is, there the vultures will gather. ^{29} "Immediately after the tribulation of those days the sun will be darkened, and the moon will not give its light, and the stars will fall from heaven, and the powers of the heavens will be shaken. ^{30} Then will appear in heaven the sign of the Son of Man, and then all the tribes of the earth will mourn, and they will see the Son of Man coming on the clouds of heaven with power and great glory. ^{31} And he will send out his angels with a loud trumpet call, and they will gather his elect from the four winds, from one end of heaven to the other.

Our first two details can be found within a single verse of this passage. Notice that this verse, listed below, is immediately before our rapture defining scripture starting in verse thirty.

Matthew 24:29
^{29} "Immediately after the tribulation of those days the sun will be darkened, and the moon will not give its light, and the stars will fall from heaven, and the powers of the heavens will be shaken.

FIVE IMPORTANT RAPTURE DETAILS

Here we are told of two things which will happen near the time of the rapture:
 1. The sun, moon, and stars will be darkened.
 2. The powers of heavenly will be shaken.

These are our first two details on the rapture. Now we will move onto rapture detail 3 which we will find by using these first two details.

Finding Rapture Detail 3

Our first two rapture details are found together in several places in scripture. The day in which these two details occur is actually given a specific name in scripture. This day is known as "The day of the Lord". We will show, in the next three verses. that the first two details are repeatedly mentioned in verses describing the day of the Lord. In the verses below our first two rapture details are underlined while the mention of the day of the Lord is highlighted.

Isaiah 13:9-13
*9 Behold, **the day of the LORD** comes, cruel, with wrath and fierce anger, to make the land a desolation and to destroy its sinners from it. 10 <u>For the stars of the heavens and their constellations will not give their light; the sun will be dark at its rising, and the moon will not shed its light.</u> 11 I will punish the world for its evil, and the wicked for their iniquity; I will put an end to the pomp of the arrogant, and lay low the pompous pride of the ruthless. 12 I will make people more rare than fine gold, and mankind than the gold of Ophir. 13 Therefore <u>I will make the heavens tremble</u>, and the earth will be shaken out of its place, at the wrath of the LORD of hosts in the day of his fierce anger.*

Joel 2:10-11
10 The earth quakes before them; <u>the heavens tremble. The sun and the moon are darkened, and the stars withdraw their shining.</u> 11 The LORD utters his voice before his army, for his

camp is exceedingly great; he who executes his word is powerful. For **the day of the LORD** is great and very awesome; who can endure it?*

Joel 3:14-16
*[14] Multitudes, multitudes, in the valley of decision! For **the day of the LORD** is near in the valley of decision. [15] <u>The sun and the moon are darkened, and the stars withdraw their shining.</u> [16] The LORD roars from Zion, and utters his voice from Jerusalem, and <u>the heavens and the earth quake.</u> But the LORD is a refuge to his people, a stronghold to the people of Israel.*

We have seen three separate times that the day of the first two rapture details is referred to as the day of the Lord. The day of the Lord is mentioned throughout both the Old and New Testaments and is the day of the rapture. The word rapture is not found in the Bible because it is not a word in the original languages the Bible was written. What we refer to as "the rapture" the Bible refers to as "the day of the Lord". We now have our third detail to help us find the location of the rapture.

3. The events of the rapture occur on a day called "The day of the Lord".

Finding Rapture Detail 4

For our fourth detail we will continue reading in Matthew 24. We have once again included our rapture defining scripture, in the first two verses, to emphasize the context of the verses we will read below.

Matthew 24:30-44
[30] Then will appear in heaven the sign of the Son of Man, and then all the tribes of the earth will mourn, and they will see the Son of Man coming on the clouds of heaven with power and great glory. [31] And he will send out his angels with a loud trumpet call, and they will gather his elect from the four

FIVE IMPORTANT RAPTURE DETAILS

winds, from one end of heaven to the other. 32 "From the fig tree learn its lesson: as soon as its branch becomes tender and puts out its leaves, you know that summer is near. 33 So also, when you see all these things, you know that he is near, at the very gates. 34 Truly, I say to you, this generation will not pass away until all these things take place. 35 Heaven and earth will pass away, but my words will not pass away. 36 "But concerning that day and hour no one knows, not even the angels of heaven, nor the Son, but the Father only. 37 For as were the days of Noah, so will be the coming of the Son of Man. 38 For as in those days before the flood they were eating and drinking, marrying and giving in marriage, until the day when Noah entered the ark, 39 and they were unaware until the flood came and swept them all away, so will be the coming of the Son of Man. 40 Then two men will be in the field; one will be taken and one left. 41 Two women will be grinding at the mill; one will be taken and one left. 42 Therefore, stay awake, for you do not know on what day your Lord is coming. 43 But know this, that if the master of the house had known in what part of the night the thief was coming, he would have stayed awake and would not have let his house be broken into. 44 Therefore you also must be ready, for the Son of Man is coming at an hour you do not expect.

There are many potential details we could examine in this passage, but the one which helps our study is found at the end of these verses.

Matthew 24:42-44
42 Therefore, stay awake, for you do not know on what day your Lord is coming. 43 But know this, that if the master of the house had known in what part of the night the thief was coming, he would have stayed awake and would not have let his house be broken into. 44 Therefore you also must be ready, for the Son of Man is coming at an hour you do not expect.

Jesus uses the allegory of a thief breaking into a house to describe the surprise which will occur at the time of His return. We will see that this reference to the day coming like a thief is repeated in other verses. Below are two verses where the day of the Lord (day of the rapture) is said to come like a thief.

2 Peter 3:10
*10 But **the day of the Lord** <u>will come like a thief,</u> and then the heavens will pass away with a roar, and the heavenly bodies will be burned up and dissolved, and the earth and the works that are done on it will be exposed.*

Joel 2:9-11
*9 They leap upon the city, they run upon the walls, they climb up into the houses, <u>they enter through the windows like a thief.</u> 10 The earth quakes before them; the heavens tremble. The sun and the moon are darkened, and the stars withdraw their shining. 11 The LORD utters his voice before his army, for his camp is exceedingly great; he who executes his word is powerful. For **the day of the LORD** is great and very awesome; who can endure it?*

The last two passages have shown the day of the Lord comes like a thief. We have also seen the day of the Lord mentioned in the New Testament for the first time. As I said before, this is the name the Bible gives to the rapture, and this name is consistent throughout both the Old and New Testaments. We now have our fourth rapture detail.

4. The day will come like a thief

Finding Rapture Detail 5

For our final detail we will reference an Old Testament verse which refers to the day of the Lord. We will see in the verse below that the day of the Lord is the day of the battle of

FIVE IMPORTANT RAPTURE DETAILS

Armageddon. We know this because Armageddon is another name for the Valley of Jehoshaphat.

Joel 3:12-16
¹² Let the nations stir themselves up and come up to the Valley of Jehoshaphat; for there I will sit to judge all the surrounding nations. ¹³ Put in the sickle, for the harvest is ripe. Go in, tread, for the winepress is full. The vats overflow, for their evil is great. ¹⁴ Multitudes, multitudes, in the valley of decision! For **the day of the LORD** is near in the valley of decision. ¹⁵ The sun and the moon are darkened, and the stars withdraw their shining. ¹⁶ The LORD roars from Zion, and utters his voice from Jerusalem, and the heavens and the earth quake. But the LORD is a refuge to his people, a stronghold to the people of Israel.

We now have the fifth detail to find the rapture in the book of Revelation.

5. The battle of Armageddon will occur.

We now have our five rapture details, and you have probably begun to realize there are many more verses in the Bible about the day of the rapture than is commonly thought. In fact, there are at least twenty-four locations in the Bible that mention the day of the Lord by name. There are full chapters in the Old Testament focusing on this day, and the entire book of Joel is a prophecy about the day of the Lord as well.

I don't believe it is an exaggeration to say this day is by far the most common event in the prophetic Old Testament. Once you learn about it you will start seeing it everywhere in scripture. You might be reading a chapter in Isaiah and suddenly realize, "Oh, this is speaking of the day of the Lord!"

I have always had an interest in what I would call the unknowns in the Bible, especially the prophetic books of the Old Testament. Many in the church ignore these books believing they are either no longer relevant, or that they are unable to be understood. I have even heard several pastors joke that these are the books where the pages of your Bible stick together. However, I had an interest in these books and believed they could be understood.

I read these books over and over and listened to recordings of them as well whenever I could. I didn't care that I couldn't understand them, I just loved the mental exercise of thinking about them. Eventually, I believe I had read and listened to them so many times that they began to make sense. I was able to group many of these prophecies into different prophetic events and eventually realized these events seemed very similar to events in Revelation.

I realized that the book of Revelation put these events in order, but the details were in the Old Testament prophecies. With that said, I can tell you we will find many details about the rapture in these prophecies. In fact, there is so much in the Bible about the day of the Lord that we will have to focus on the rapture while leaving the other details for a book I will write at a later date.

Listing Our Five Details

Let's list all five of the details of the rapture we will use to find the event in Revelation.
1. The sun, moon, and stars will be darkened.
2. The powers of heaven will be shaken.
3. The events of the rapture occur on a day scripture calls "The day of the Lord".
4. The day will come like a thief.
5. The battle of Armageddon will occur.

We will soon find where all these details occur in Revelation. However, we will first tie together our two rapture defining scriptures to ensure both are actually speaking of the same event.

3

Linking Our Rapture Defining Scriptures

We will tie our two rapture defining scriptures together by showing that each occurs on the day of the Lord. Before we begin, I want to discuss how to find answers to questions like this in scripture. Let me give an example of another question I was once trying to answer. I was once wondering why Jesus gave the answer he did in the following verse.

Matthew 12:7
And if you had known what this means, 'I desire mercy, not sacrifice,' you would not have condemned the guiltless.

This answer seemed to me to be out of character for Jesus, and I spent quite some time thinking about it. Why did Jesus speak against them when they were ignorant of their sin? Couldn't Jesus have just explained to them why they were wrong? Later, I found the answer just a few chapters back where Jesus spoke to the same people for making the same mistake.

THE UNKNOWN RAPTURE SCRIPTURES

Matthew 9:13
Go and learn what this means: 'I desire mercy, and not sacrifice.' For I came not to call the righteous, but sinners."

Here Jesus instructs the same group of people to learn what this phrase means. In chapter 12 he is harsher with them since they obviously made no effort to learn the meaning of this phrase. Ignoring what Jesus had already told them caused them to make the same mistake.

The way to find the answer to my question was to read a broader section of the book. This is often the best way to find answers in the Bible, but this method is not used often enough. Imagine you were in a group discussing this verse in Matthew 12:7. How do you think the participants would seek to answer the question of why Jesus gave this reply? From my experience the answers would probably look something like this:

- Well God is sovereign, and He knew the best way to answer.
- Jesus knew their hearts were evil so he spoke against their sin.
- Jesus is full of justice and must speak against sin.

Many answers like these would likely be given with no real effort to read more of the surrounding verses. One issue that often arises in discussions like these is the assumption that the answer is much more complex than is really the case. People give a broad, almost philosophical answer, thinking any answer beyond that is some form of advanced calculus. In reality, the answer is often in addition, as in the addition of a few more verses. However, they believe the answer is so complex that the simple answer is not even noticed.

After no detailed answer is found in these discussions someone will usually end the discussion, perhaps quoting this verse:

LINKING OUR RAPTURE DEFINING SCRIPTURES

1 Corinthians 2:9 (KJV)
⁹ But as it is written, Eye hath not seen, nor ear heard, neither have entered into the heart of man, the things which God hath prepared for them that love him.

In other words, they would be saying this is one of those things no one can understand. This is the polite way many in the church say, "If I can't figure this out then God obviously never intended it to be found out." Many believers come to this conclusion after about 5 minutes of study. The sad thing is that once you reach this conclusion you stop looking for the answer.

Even this verse, which many of you have probably heard repeated many times, is often used incorrectly. Let's see what happens when we add the very next verse.

1 Corinthians 2:9-10
⁹ But, as it is written, "What no eye has seen, nor ear heard, nor the heart of man imagined, what God has prepared for those who love him"— ¹⁰ these things God has revealed to us through the Spirit. For the Spirit searches everything, even the depths of God.

As you can see reading the very next verse changes everything. Many false doctrines throughout church history would likely have never existed if their creators had bothered to read the two or three verses before and after the scriptures used to justify their beliefs.

Now back to our main topic for this chapter. We want to prove our two rapture defining scriptures are speaking of the same event. We will accomplish this by showing they both occur on the day of the Lord. We have already proven our rapture defining scripture in Matthew occurs on this day, so we only need to prove 1 Thessalonians 4:16-17 occurs on the day of the Lord.

Quite a few theologians believe this passage is separate from the day of the Lord, but I do not have to contest this belief. You the reader can do it for me! Grab your Bible or find one online and open to 1 Thessalonians 4:16-17. Think about what I have written in this chapter relating to finding answers in scripture, and prove that these verses occur on the day of the Lord. This may sound like a joke, but I want you to see how easy finding answers in scripture can be when you use the right methods. I will of course give a detailed answer below, but I encourage you to spend at least one minute looking for the answer yourself. Stop reading here until after you do this.

Do some of you have an answer to challenge those theologians who believe those verses do not speak of the day of the Lord? Let's read the five verses following this passage to get our answer.

1 Thessalonians 4:16-18
16 For the Lord himself will descend from heaven with a cry of command, with the voice of an archangel, and with the sound of the trumpet of God. And the dead in Christ will rise first. 17 Then we who are alive, who are left, will be caught up together with them in the clouds to meet the Lord in the air, and so we will always be with the Lord. 18 Therefore encourage one another with these words.

This is our rapture defining scripture with verse 18 included. Showing that this event and the day of the Lord are the same is as simple as reading the next few verses. Verse 18 is the last verse of chapter 4, but the author continues speaking of this same event in the next chapter. It is important to remember that the chapters and verses were not added until over 1000 years after this book was written. With this in mind, let's read the next four verses.

1 Thessalonians 5:1-4
Now concerning the times and the seasons, brothers, you have no need to have anything written to you. ² For you yourselves are fully aware that **the day of the Lord** <u>will come like a thief in the night.</u> *³ While people are saying, "There is peace and*

LINKING OUR RAPTURE DEFINING SCRIPTURES

security," then sudden destruction will come upon them as labor pains come upon a pregnant woman, and they will not escape. ⁴ But you are not in darkness, brothers, for that day to surprise you <u>like a thief</u>.

As you can see. 1 Thessalonians 4:16-17 is speaking of the day of the Lord. For even more confirmation we are also given our rapture detail relating to the day coming like a thief. To be fair, most theologians are not ignorant of the fact that the day of the Lord is mentioned here. Most of them will find some way to explain that Paul actually changes topics between chapters 4-5. However, we will address these same verses later in the book when we have much more evidence, and this will be proven very conclusively.

I know some of you found this answer, but if you did not do not worry. Stopping at the end of a chapter is a very common mistake. Always remember to search for answers in the Bible by starting with simple methods like this.

In this chapter we have connected our two rapture defining scriptures through the day of the Lord. Now that we have confirmed both scriptures are speaking of the same event, we will use our five rapture details to find the rapture in the book of Revelation.

4

Finding Our Rapture Details in Revelation

We have a list of five details which we know happen on the day of the rapture. As a reminder, here they are once again:

1. The sun, moon, and stars will be darkened.
2. The powers of heaven will be shaken.
3. The events of the rapture occur on a day scripture calls "The day of the Lord".
4. The day will come like a thief.
5. The battle of Armageddon will occur.

All five of these details can be found in the book of Revelation. More importantly, all five details can be found within nine verses of each other! All five of the details are underlined in these nine verses below.

Revelation 16:10-18
¹⁰ The fifth angel poured out his bowl on the throne of the beast, and <u>its kingdom was plunged into darkness.</u> People gnawed their tongues in anguish ¹¹ and cursed the God of heaven for their pain and sores. They did not repent of their

FINDING RAPTURE DETAILS IN REVELATION

deeds. ¹² *The sixth angel poured out his bowl on the great river Euphrates, and its water was dried up, to prepare the way for the kings from the east.* ¹³ *And I saw, coming out of the mouth of the dragon and out of the mouth of the beast and out of the mouth of the false prophet, three unclean spirits like frogs.* ¹⁴ *For they are demonic spirits, performing signs, who go abroad to the kings of the whole world, to assemble them for battle on <u>the great day of God the Almighty</u>.* ¹⁵ *(<u>"Behold, I am coming like a thief</u>! Blessed is the one who stays awake, keeping his garments on, that he may not go about naked and be seen exposed!")* ¹⁶ <u>*And they assembled them at the place that in Hebrew is called Armageddon.*</u> ¹⁷ *The seventh angel poured out his bowl into the air, and a loud voice came out of the temple, from the throne, saying, "It is done!"* ¹⁸ *And there were flashes of lightning, rumblings, peals of thunder, and <u>a great earthquake such as there had never been since man was on the earth, so great was that earthquake.</u>*

We have found all five of our rapture details in this passage. Here is where each detail was found.

1. The sun, moon, and stars will be darkened.
   (Revelation 16:10)
2. The powers of heaven will be shaken.
   (Revelation 16:18)
3. The events of the rapture occur on a day scripture calls "The day of the Lord".
   (Revelation 16:14)
4. The day will come like a thief.
   (Revelation 16:15)
5. The battle of Armageddon will occur.
   (Revelation 16:16)

All evidence so far points to Revelation 16 as the location of the rapture. We would be done our investigation if it weren't for one major issue: there is no mention of the Lord coming on the clouds. We now need to prove this happens at the same time as these five details.

Before we go to the next step, I want to point out that we have come to the spot we are now without doing anything with much difficulty. The only things we have done are to list five details occurring around the time of the rapture, find those same five details in the book of Revelation, and of course we read the next five verses after our rapture defining scripture in 1 Thessalonians 4:16-17. This has not been rocket science. Even so, we already have a good idea of where the rapture occurs in Revelation, a feat many believe is impossible. If it is really so simple to reach this point, then why has this remained a mystery for all these years? I believe there are two main reasons for this which we will discuss:

1. Over Reverence for Traditional Interpretations
2. False Belief the Answer Cannot Be Found

Over Reverence for Traditional Interpretations

I will tell you a secret. If you make a serious effort to study the rapture you will notice many contradictions within traditional rapture teachings. What do you do when you find these contradictions? Most take the wrong approach. It is easy to think things like, "A traditional belief like this can't be wrong", or "There must be something here I don't understand". Either of these responses could have merit, but you have an over reverence for traditional interpretations if you stop your investigation after having these thoughts.

Just how old are these "traditional beliefs" about the rapture? You may be surprised to learn the current rapture theory, that separates the rapture from Jesus' second coming, did not exist before the 1800's. This is not a belief that has existed for 2000 years as many might expect. This does not date back to beliefs such as Jesus being the Son of God or eternal life through making Jesus your Lord and has not been tested as those beliefs have. Did all the believers over the course of almost 1800 years just not see this theory, or is it possible the

FINDING RAPTURE DETAILS IN REVELATION

theory may have some problems with it? Any contradictions we find are clearly worth investigating.

Ignoring contradictions you find within a theory causes you to have a blind spot. When I was first learning to read I passed a "no smoking" sign several times each week which had a space in the wrong location. It read, "nosmo king". I didn't think much about it and just assumed "nosmo" was a word I had not yet learned. I continued to see this sign several times each week all the way until I was in second or third grade. Almost anyone in second or third grade could look at that sign and instantly realize it said, "no smoking". However, I had become trapped in the opinion I had formed several years earlier believing that nosmo was a word I had not yet learned. This blinded me from seeing the obvious truth.

This same type of blindness comes from having an over reverence for the first theory you hear about any part of the Bible. If you refuse to bend it won't matter how obvious the counter evidence becomes. At some point you need to stop blindly following the theory and examine the evidence for yourself. When I was in second or third grade I finally decided to figure out the meaning of the "nosmo king" sign. After examining it for a short time I was able to see the truth. In the same way I hope all of you reading this book will closely examine the scriptures and interpretations presented, giving them a fair evaluation, without running them through the filter of traditional interpretations.

False Belief the Answer Cannot Be Found

Now onto the second reason I believe the rapture has remained a mystery for so long. I spoke in the last chapter about how many believers, sometimes after only 5 minutes, determine the answer to something in scripture cannot be found. You often hear people say something along the lines of, "I guess that's something we won't know until we get to heaven." This seems to be a rather common opinion about anything which might be considered difficult to understand.

However, here is what the Bible says related to knowing the mysteries of God.

1 Corinthians 2:9-16
9 But, as it is written, "What no eye has seen, nor ear heard, nor the heart of man imagined, what God has prepared for those who love him"— 10 these things God has revealed to us through the Spirit. For the Spirit searches everything, even the depths of God. 11 For who knows a person's thoughts except the spirit of that person, which is in him? So also no one comprehends the thoughts of God except the Spirit of God. 12 Now we have received not the spirit of the world, but the Spirit who is from God, that we might understand the things freely given us by God. 13 And we impart this in words not taught by human wisdom but taught by the Spirit, interpreting spiritual truths to those who are spiritual. 14 The natural person does not accept the things of the Spirit of God, for they are folly to him, and he is not able to understand them because they are spiritually discerned. 15 The spiritual person judges all things, but is himself to be judged by no one. 16 "For who has understood the mind of the Lord so as to instruct him?" But we have the mind of Christ.

Here are some things said in this passage:
1. *"What no eye has seen, nor ear heard, nor the heart of man imagined, what God has prepared for those who love him"— 10 these things God has revealed to us through the Spirit.*
2. *Now we have received not the spirit of the world, but the Spirit who is from God, that we might understand the things freely given us by God.*
3. *"For who has understood the mind of the Lord so as to instruct him?" But we have the mind of Christ.*

Two of the three points above mention that the Holy Spirit, specifically that He will reveal the mysteries of God to us. This section of scripture is not alone in telling us this truth.

FINDING RAPTURE DETAILS IN REVELATION

Jesus himself said the same thing about the Holy Spirit in the next passage.

John 16:12-15
12 "I still have many things to say to you, but you cannot bear them now. 13 When the Spirit of truth comes, he will guide you into all the truth, for he will not speak on his own authority, but whatever he hears he will speak, and he will declare to you the things that are to come. 14 He will glorify me, for <u>he will take what is mine and declare it to you.</u> 15 <u>All that the Father has is mine; therefore I said that he will take what is mine and declare it to you.</u>

This verse makes it plain that there are no limits to the knowledge we can receive through the Holy Spirit. Jesus tells us that all that the Father has will be made known to us through the Spirit. However, there is something we must do to receive this knowledge. This is shown in the next passage.

James 1:5-8
5 If any of you lacks wisdom, let him ask God, who gives generously to all without reproach, and it will be given him. 6 But let him ask in faith, with no doubting, for the one who doubts is like a wave of the sea that is driven and tossed by the wind. 7 For that person must not suppose that he will receive anything from the Lord; 8 he is a double-minded man, unstable in all his ways.

In this last passage we see once again that God will give us all knowledge, although this verse also makes clear we will only receive this knowledge if we believe God will give it to us. The moment we doubt a solution can be found we disqualify ourselves from the help the Holy Spirit can give us. In this case we would never find a solution, just as we have chosen to believe. In other words, if you decide you won't know something until you get to heaven then the Holy Spirit will not give you that knowledge.

THE UNKNOWN RAPTURE SCRIPTURES

When I first prayed for knowledge on Revelation this is a lesson God kept hammering into my head again and again. It is a necessary step to obtaining wisdom in the things of God. With this in mind, we should decide with certainty that we can fully understand the rapture. Let's not limit ourselves in our thinking and disqualify ourselves from allowing the Holy Spirit to help us find the truth.

Let's get back to our study. We have found our five rapture details, occurring near the time of the rapture, in Revelation 16. However, we have not found the rapture itself. We will now show that the extent of the day of Lord (day of the rapture), in Revelation, stretches through several chapters. This will give us our window to find the rapture.

5

The Six Chapters of the Rapture

We have shown that our two rapture defining scriptures are speaking of the day of the Lord. We have even found five events from this day in Revelation 16:10-18. However, we have left out the most important part. I am speaking of the event mentioned in our two rapture defining scriptures below where the Lord comes on the clouds.

1 Thessalonians 4:16-17
<u>16 For the Lord himself will descend from heaven</u> *with a cry of command, with the voice of an archangel, and with the sound of the trumpet of God. And the dead in Christ will rise first. 17 Then we who are alive, who are left, will be caught up together with them in the clouds to meet the Lord in the air, and so we will always be with the Lord.*

Matthew 24:30-31
30 Then will appear in heaven the sign of the Son of Man, and then all the tribes of the earth will mourn, and <u>they will see the Son of Man coming on the clouds of heaven</u> with power

and great glory. ³¹ And he will send out his angels with a loud trumpet call, and they will gather his elect from the four winds, from one end of heaven to the other.

If we have truly found all the events surrounding the rapture in Revelation 16:10-18, why isn't this event included? The answer is that the day of the Lord is not contained in a single chapter of Revelation. In fact, Revelation 14-19 all occurs on a single day, that being the day of the Lord or the day of the rapture.

To avoid doubling the size of this book we will limit ourselves, in most cases, to showing just one point in each of these chapters that can be linked to the day of the Lord. That will be sufficient to prove these chapters occur on the day of the rapture.

Revelation 14

We will start our study into what chapters in Revelation occur on the day of the Lord in Revelation 14. Here is the section of scripture we will use to show the day of the Lord occurs in this chapter.

Revelation 14:17-20
¹⁷ Then another angel came out of the temple in heaven, and he too had a sharp sickle. ¹⁸ And another angel came out from the altar, the angel who has authority over the fire, and he called with a loud voice to the one who had the sharp sickle, "Put in your sickle and gather the clusters from the vine of the earth, for its grapes are ripe." ¹⁹ So the angel swung his sickle across the earth and gathered the grape harvest of the earth and threw it into the great winepress of the wrath of God. ²⁰ And the winepress was trodden outside the city, and blood flowed from the winepress, as high as a horse's bridle, for 1,600 stadia.

THE SIX CHAPTERS OF THE RAPTURE

This event is also mentioned in the book of Joel. In this Old Testament passage, we are also told this event occurs on the day of the Lord.

Joel 3:12-13
*¹² Let the nations stir themselves up and come up to the Valley of Jehoshaphat; for there I will sit to judge all the surrounding nations. ¹³ <u>Put in the sickle, for the harvest is ripe. Go in, tread, for the winepress is full. The vats overflow, for their evil is great.</u> ¹⁴ Multitudes, multitudes, in the valley of decision! For **the day of the LORD** is near in the valley of decision. ¹⁵ The sun and the moon are darkened, and the stars withdraw their shining. ¹⁶ The LORD roars from Zion, and utters his voice from Jerusalem, and the heavens and the earth quake. But the LORD is a refuge to his people, a stronghold to the people of Israel.*

This verse directly mentions the day of the Lord, including several details we have seen happen on this day (sun, moon, and stars darkened and heavens and earth shake). In the underlined section above, it also references the same event which happens in Revelation 14:17-20. Let's list the similarities between Revelation 14:17-20 and Joel 3:12-13:

1. A sickle is used to harvest.
2. Grapes are harvested (we know this since Joel 3:13 speaks of wine.)
3. The grapes are trodden in a winepress.
4. The trodden grapes are referred to as people.

By comparing the similarities of these two sections of scripture we can see they seem to be speaking of the same event. Later in the book, we will revisit this comparison to conclusively show the events are the same. This appears to show Revelation 14 occurs on the day of the Lord, but since this is not completely conclusive, at this time, we will give another example.

Another quick way to show this chapter speaks of the day of Jesus' return is to look at the first verse in the chapter. In this verse Jesus is already standing on the ground, meaning this must be the day of His return.

Revelation 14:1
Then I looked, and behold, on Mount Zion stood the Lamb, and with him 144,000 who had his name and his Father's name written on their foreheads.

Here we see Jesus standing on the earth. If He is already standing on the earth we know this must be occurring on the day of His return, meaning the day of the Lord.

Revelation 15 and 16

Now we will show Revelation 15-16 occur on the day of the Lord. Revelation 15 and 16 both deal with the seven bowls of God's wrath. In chapter fifteen the bowls are passed out, and in chapter sixteen the bowls are poured upon the earth. Remember that we found our five rapture details in Revelation 16. Here is that passage once again with the mention of the day of the Lord underlined.

Revelation 16:10-18
[10] The fifth angel poured out his bowl on the throne of the beast, and its kingdom was plunged into darkness. People gnawed their tongues in anguish [11] and cursed the God of heaven for their pain and sores. They did not repent of their deeds. [12] The sixth angel poured out his bowl on the great river Euphrates, and its water was dried up, to prepare the way for the kings from the east. [13] And I saw, coming out of the mouth of the dragon and out of the mouth of the beast and out of the mouth of the false prophet, three unclean spirits like frogs. [14] For they are demonic spirits, performing signs, who go abroad to the kings of the whole world, to assemble them for battle <u>on the great day of God the Almighty.</u> [15] ("Behold, I am coming like a thief! Blessed is the one who stays awake,

THE SIX CHAPTERS OF THE RAPTURE

keeping his garments on, that he may not go about naked and be seen exposed!") [16] And they assembled them at the place that in Hebrew is called Armageddon. [17] The seventh angel poured out his bowl into the air, and a loud voice came out of the temple, from the throne, saying, "It is done!" [18] And there were flashes of lightning, rumblings, peals of thunder, and a great earthquake such as there had never been since man was on the earth, so great was that earthquake.

This proves at least part of Revelation 16 occurs on the day of the Lord. Now, what about chapter 15. It is difficult to prove this chapter occurs on the day of the Lord since it is so short. In this chapter, the seven bowls are passed out to the angels who will pour them upon the earth. Notice below that the bowls are poured out on the earth immediately after they are passed out.

Revelation 15:7-8 – Revelation 16:1-2a
[7] And one of the four living creatures gave to the seven angels seven golden bowls full of the wrath of God who lives forever and ever, [8] and the sanctuary was filled with smoke from the glory of God and from his power, and no one could enter the sanctuary until the seven plagues of the seven angels were finished. (chapter 16) *Then I heard a loud voice from the temple telling the seven angels, "Go and pour out on the earth the seven bowls of the wrath of God." [2] So the first angel went and poured out his bowl on the earth,*

We can see the first bowl is poured out upon the earth immediately after it is passed out. Since this is the case, we can prove chapter 15 occurs on the day of the Lord if we can prove all seven bowls are poured upon the earth in a single day. We have already shown, from our passage above, that bowls five through seven are poured out on the day of the Lord, so it is certainly believable that all might be poured on the day. To prove this, we will use the following process:

Step 1. We will link God's wrath to the day of the Lord.
Step 2. We will investigate the purpose of God's wrath on the day of the Lord.
Step 3. We will find a verse which tells us that the purpose for God's wrath on the day of the Lord will occur in a single day.

Step 1.
In our first step we will link God's wrath to the day of the Lord. We will look at two verses which refer to the day of the Lord as a day of wrath. In the two verses below the mention of the day of the Lord is highlighted while the mentions of wrath are underlined.

Isaiah 13:9-13
9 Behold, **the day of the LORD** *comes, <u>cruel, with wrath and fierce anger, to make the land a desolation and to destroy its sinners from it.</u> 10 For the stars of the heavens and their constellations will not give their light; the sun will be dark at its rising, and the moon will not shed its light. 11 I will punish the world for its evil, and the wicked for their iniquity; I will put an end to the pomp of the arrogant, and lay low the pompous pride of the ruthless. 12 I will make people more rare than fine gold, and mankind than the gold of Ophir. 13 Therefore I will make the heavens tremble, and the earth will be shaken out of its place, <u>at the wrath of the LORD of hosts in the day of his fierce anger.</u>*

Zephaniah 1:14-18
14 **The great day of the LORD** *is near, near and hastening fast; the sound of* **the day of the LORD** *is bitter; the mighty man cries aloud there. 15 <u>A day of wrath is that day</u>, a day of distress and anguish, a day of ruin and devastation, a day of darkness and gloom, a day of clouds and thick darkness, 16 a day of trumpet blast and battle cry against the fortified cities and against the lofty battlements. 17 I will bring distress on mankind, so that they shall walk like the blind, because they*

have sinned against the LORD; their blood shall be poured out like dust, and their flesh like dung. ¹⁸ *Neither their silver nor their gold shall be able to deliver them on <u>the day of the wrath of the LORD.</u> In the fire of his jealousy, all the earth shall be consumed; for a full and sudden end he will make of all the inhabitants of the earth.*

We can see that God's wrath clearly plays a role on the day of the Lord.

Step 2.
In our next step we will find the purpose of God's wrath on the day of the Lord. We can find a reason listed in one of the verses we read in step 1. Here it is again.

Isaiah 13:9
⁹ *Behold, the day of the LORD comes, cruel, with wrath and fierce anger, to make the land a desolation and <u>to destroy its sinners from it</u>.*

We can see that the wrath of the Lord will destroy sin from the earth. Let's examine Revelation 15 to see that this is accomplished by the seven bowls.

Revelation 15:7-8
⁷ *And one of the four living creatures gave to the seven angels seven golden bowls full of the wrath of God who lives forever and ever,* ⁸ *and the sanctuary was filled with smoke from the glory of God and from his power, and no one could enter the sanctuary until the seven plagues of the seven angels were finished.*

This verse initiates the pouring of the seven bowls of God's wrath. Let's look at another place in the Bible where God wraps himself inside a cloud and pours out his wrath. This will help us understand the purpose of the cloud (smoke).

THE UNKNOWN RAPTURE SCRIPTURES

Lamentations 3:41-44
⁴¹ Let us lift up our hearts and hands to God in heaven: ⁴² "We have transgressed and rebelled, and you have not forgiven. ⁴³ "You have wrapped yourself with anger and pursued us, killing without pity; ⁴⁴ <u>*you have wrapped yourself with a cloud so that no prayer can pass through.*</u>

We can see that the purpose of the cloud (smoke) covering God's sanctuary in Revelation 15 is to prevent prayers from being made for those being destroyed on the earth. We can also see in the verse above that the reason for those being destroyed is sin (*⁴² "We have transgressed and rebelled, and you have not forgiven.*) This is echoed in the next verse where, once again, no prayers are accepted for those being destroyed when God pours out His wrath on the earth.

Jeremiah 7:16-20
¹⁶ "As for you, <u>*do not pray for this people, or lift up a cry or prayer for them, and do not intercede with me, for I will not hear you.*</u> *¹⁷ Do you not see what they are doing in the cities of Judah and in the streets of Jerusalem? ¹⁸ The children gather wood, the fathers kindle fire, and the women knead dough, to make cakes for the queen of heaven. And they pour out drink offerings to other gods, to provoke me to anger. ¹⁹ Is it I whom they provoke? declares the LORD. Is it not themselves, to their own shame? ²⁰ Therefore thus says the Lord GOD: Behold,* <u>*my anger and my wrath will be poured out on this place*</u>*, upon man and beast, upon the trees of the field and the fruit of the ground; it will burn and not be quenched."*

We see once again that God's wrath is poured out to eliminate sin. We have seen a theme throughout the Bible telling us what occurs when God's patience with sin comes to an end. At that point, God pours out His wrath to completely destroy the sin, and will accept no intercession for those receiving the judgment.

THE SIX CHAPTERS OF THE RAPTURE

We can see from the events surrounding the distribution of the bowls of God's wrath that they are meant to destroy the sin of the land. We can confirm the seven bowls of God's wrath accomplish this task by looking back at Revelation 15, since it tells us directly that the seven bowls will complete God's wrath.

Revelation 15:1
Then I saw another sign in heaven, great and amazing, seven angels with seven plagues, which are the last, for <u>with them the wrath of God is finished.</u>

If all wrath is finished, then all sin is destroyed.

Step 3.
We have seen in the first two steps that the day of the Lord is the day of God's wrath and that the wrath of the Lord will destroy all the sin on the earth. The next verse tells us God plans to destroy all sin (iniquity) on a single day.

Zechariah 3:8-9
⁸ Hear now, O Joshua the high priest, you and your friends who sit before you, for they are men who are a sign: behold, I will bring my servant the Branch. ⁹ For behold, on the stone that I have set before Joshua, on a single stone with seven eyes, I will engrave its inscription, declares the LORD of hosts, and <u>I will remove the iniquity of this land in a single day.</u>

The seven bowls of God's wrath are meant to destroy all sin throughout the earth. The last verse tells us God will remove all iniquity from the land in a single day. We will revisit this verse later in this book to prove it is speaking of the day of the Lord, but for now all that is important is that all sin is destroyed in a day. From this we know all seven bowls occur on a single day. Since our five rapture details occur during these bowls, and the day of the Lord is also mentioned directly in Revelation 16, we know all the bowls are poured out on the day of the Lord. Since the first bowl is poured out immediately after the angels receive the bowls in chapter 15, we know this chapter occurs on the day of the Lord as well. This proves that Revelation 15-16 occur on the day of the Lord. We will get confirmation the bowls occur in a single day in our investigation of Revelation 17-18.

Revelation 17 and 18

Now we will prove Revelation 17-18 occurs on the day of the Lord. Revelation 17 and 18 both deal with the destruction of Babylon the Great. An extremely oversimplified definition of Babylon the Great is to call it as the evil kingdom controlling the earth at the time of Jesus' return. We will leave it at that, since we only need to prove these chapters occur on the day of the Lord. At the end of Revelation 16 we are told the judgment upon Babylon the great occurs during the seventh bowl of God's wrath.

Revelation 16:17-21
17 The seventh angel poured out his bowl into the air, and a loud voice came out of the temple, from the throne, saying, "It is done!" 18 And there were flashes of lightning, rumblings peals of thunder, and a great earthquake such as there had never been since man was on the earth, so great was that earthquake. 19 The great city was split into three parts, and the cities of the nations fell, and <u>God remembered Babylon the great, to make her drain the cup of the wine of the fury of his wrath.</u> 20 And every island fled away, and no mountains were to be found. 21 And great hailstones, about one hundred pounds each, fell from heaven on people; and they cursed God for the plague of the hail, because the plague was so severe.

As you can see, judgment is poured upon Babylon the Great during this bowl. Immediately after this bowl John is told to witness the destruction on Babylon. This brings us into Revelation 17-18.

THE SIX CHAPTERS OF THE RAPTURE

Revelation 17:1-5
<u>Then one of the seven angels who had the seven bowls came and said to me, "Come, I will show you the judgment of the great prostitute who is seated on many waters,</u> ² with whom the kings of the earth have committed sexual immorality, and with the wine of whose sexual immorality the dwellers on earth have become drunk." ³ And he carried me away in the Spirit into a wilderness, and I saw a woman sitting on a scarlet beast that was full of blasphemous names, and it had seven heads and ten horns. ⁴ The woman was arrayed in purple and scarlet, and adorned with gold and jewels and pearls, holding in her hand a golden cup full of abominations and the impurities of her sexual immorality. ⁵ <u>And on her forehead was written a name of mystery: "Babylon the great,</u> mother of prostitutes and of earth's abominations."

We know the destruction of Babylon the Great happens on the day of the Lord since it occurs at the seventh bowl of God's wrath. We have already proven this bowl occurs on the day. However, there are two chapters full of the sins and destruction of Babylon the Great. Does all of this really occur in one day? We are actually directly told it does.

Revelation 18:8
⁸ For this reason <u>her plagues will come in a single day</u>, death and mourning and famine, and she will be burned up with fire; for mighty is the Lord God who has judged her."

From this we know Revelation 17-18 occurs on the day of the Lord. This also confirms all seven bowls of God's wrath are poured out in a single day.

Revelation 19

Revelation 19 begins with a celebration of the destruction of Babylon the Great, which we know occurs on the day of the Lord.

THE UNKNOWN RAPTURE SCRIPTURES

Revelation 19:1-3
After this I heard what seemed to be the loud voice of a great multitude in heaven, crying out, "Hallelujah! Salvation and glory and power belong to our God, ²for his judgments are true and just; for he has judged the great prostitute who corrupted the earth with her immorality, and has avenged on her the blood of his servants." ³Once more they cried out, "Hallelujah! The smoke from her goes up forever and ever."

We know this celebration must be on the same day as Babylon's destruction, since they would not wait until the next day to celebrate. So, we know this chapter is within the timeframe of the day of the Lord as well.

We have now proven Revelation 14-19 occurs on the day of the Lord

6

Purposing an Exact Rapture Location in Revelation

We now know the rapture occurs somewhere within the chapters of Revelation 14-19. We now need to find a potential location within these chapters which we can investigate. We must find a location in Revelation 14-19 that appears similar to our rapture defining scriptures. There is, in fact, a section in our window that is similar. Let's read our two rapture defining scriptures again, while taking note of the underlined section in each.

1 Thessalonians 4:16-17
[16] For the Lord himself will descend from heaven with a cry of command, with the voice of an archangel, and with the sound of the trumpet of God. And the dead in Christ will rise first. [17] Then we who are alive, who are left, will be <u>caught up together with them in the clouds to meet the Lord in the air</u>, and so we will always be with the Lord.

THE UNKNOWN RAPTURE SCRIPTURES

Matthew 24:30-31
³⁰ Then will appear in heaven the sign of the Son of Man, and then all the tribes of the earth will mourn, and <u>they will see the Son of Man coming on the clouds</u> of heaven with power and great glory. ³¹ And he will send out his angels with a loud trumpet call, and they will gather his elect from the four winds, from one end of heaven to the other.

The two passages both speak of the son of man (or Lord) coming on the clouds. We can find a similar reference to the son of man coming on the clouds within Revelation 14, which is within our window.

Revelation 14:14-16
¹⁴ Then I looked, and behold, <u>a white cloud</u>, and <u>seated on the cloud one like a son of man</u>, with a golden crown on his head, and a sharp sickle in his hand. ¹⁵ And another angel came out of the temple, calling with a loud voice to him who sat on the cloud, "Put in your sickle, and reap, for the hour to reap has come, for the harvest of the earth is fully ripe." ¹⁶ So he who sat on the cloud swung his sickle across the earth, and the earth was reaped.

This verse is similar enough to our rapture defining scriptures to deserve an investigation. The reference to the son of man coming on the clouds is too much of a coincidence to ignore. However, there are also some differences. Our rapture defining scriptures refer to the sign of the son of man while our purposed rapture location refers to "one like a son of man". It would clearly be wrong to just assume this verse is speaking of the same event with differences like these. We will need a thorough investigation before we come to that conclusion.

In order to accomplish this investigation, we will break down our rapture defining scriptures into four parts: The sign of the son of man, the voice of the archangel, the trumpet call, and the rapture itself.

PURPOSING A RAPTURE LOCATION

Purposed Rapture Location
Revelation 14:14-16

	1 Thessalonians 4:13-17 (Rapture Defining Scripture)	Matthew 24:30-31 (Rapture Defining Scripture)	Revelation 14:14-16 (Purposed Rapture Location in Revelation)
Sign of the son of man	¹³ But we do not want you to be uninformed, brothers, about those who are asleep, that you may not grieve as others do who have no hope. ¹⁴ For since we believe that Jesus died and rose again, even so, through Jesus, God will bring with him those who have fallen asleep. ¹⁵ For this we declare to you by a word from the Lord, that we who are alive, who are left until the coming of the Lord, will not precede those who have fallen asleep.	³⁰ Then will appear in heaven the sign of the Son of Man, and then all the tribes of the earth will mourn, and they will see the Son of Man coming on the clouds of heaven with power and great glory.	¹⁴ Then I looked, and behold, a white cloud, and seated on the cloud one like a son of man, with a golden crown on his head, and a sharp sickle in his hand.
Voice of the archangel	¹⁶ For the Lord himself will descend from heaven with a cry of command, with the voice of an archangel,	(not given)	¹⁵ And another angel came out of the temple, calling with a loud voice to him who sat on the cloud, "Put in your sickle, and reap, for the hour to reap has come, for the harvest of the earth is fully ripe."
Trumpet call	and with the sound of the trumpet of God.	³¹ And he will send out his angels with a loud trumpet call,	(not given)
The saints "caught up" (rapture)	And the dead in Christ will rise first. ¹⁷ Then we who are alive, who are left, will be caught up together with them in the clouds to meet the Lord in the air, and so we will always be with the Lord.	and they will gather his elect from the four winds, from one end of heaven to the other.	¹⁶ So he who sat on the cloud swung his sickle across the earth, and the earth was reaped.

THE UNKNOWN RAPTURE SCRIPTURES

Each of the next four chapters will examine one of these four aspects of our rapture defining scriptures. You can get an idea of what we will be doing by examining the table on the previous page. Each row in the table will get its own chapter and we will prove each part of the rapture recorded in our rapture defining scriptures is fulfilled in our purposed rapture location in Revelation 14:14-16. Once all of this is proven we will confidently know exactly where the rapture occurs in the book of Revelation.

Before we go forward let's have a quick review of what we have accomplished so far. First, we chose the two verses most commonly believed to be speaking of the rapture, as our starting point, naming them our rapture defining scriptures. Second, we found five details occurring around the time of our rapture defining scripture in Matthew. We showed the verse immediately before this rapture defining scripture occurred on a day called the day of the Lord. Third, we examined our other rapture defining scripture and confirmed it also occurred on the day of the Lord. This confirmed our two rapture defining scriptures were really the same event. Fourth, we found our five rapture details listed within nine verses of each other in Revelation 16. The day of the Lord was even directly mentioned. However, the actual rapture was not seen so we had to continue deeper. Fifth, we proved the day of the Lord stretched from Revelation 14-19. This told us that all these chapters occurred on the day of the rapture. Sixth, we found a location in Revelation 14, which we know occurs on the day of the rapture, which appears similar to our two rapture defining scriptures. Seventh, we are about to examine Revelation 14:14-16 in detail, using the table on the previous page, to determine if it really is the raptures location in Revelation.

If you understand the last paragraph you understand the entire process of this book. Accomplishing all these steps from scratch is by no means easy, but understanding the process is very easy once all the steps have been completed. With that said, if you disagree with any part of this interpretation I

PURPOSING A RAPTURE LOCATION

encourage you to go back through our steps and determine where you believe I made a mistake.

However, some of you may have concerns that cannot be answered in this way. As an example, take our study in which we proved that the day of the Lord is the same day spoken of in 1 Thessalonians 4:16-17. Many Bible scholars are not ignorant of the fact that the day of the Lord is mentioned five verses ahead. However, many believe chapter 5 starts a different topic. One theory goes that Paul is answering multiple questions in a row the Thessalonians have written to him without fully restating their questions. Paul is beginning another answer in chapter 5 so the day of the Lord is mentioned separately from the previous chapter.

This theory and other unmentioned theories are certainly worthy to be tested. However, a theory like the one listed above is almost impossible to either prove or disprove directly. We need another method. Fortunately for us, our method of interpretation almost eliminates the need to test any of these theories. In our examination of the table shown earlier we are going to link 1 Thessalonians 4:16-17 to both Matthew 24:30-31 and to the day of the Lord quite a few times. To quote myself from earlier in the book, "If we can read ten separate verses in the Bible that all say the same thing we will not be fooled when told one of those ten verses means something different." With all the links we will be finding in scripture the previous theory falls apart. That explanation will not be valid for all the links we will find.

To state this another way, we will not be attempting to disprove the many theories which contrast ours. Instead, we will seek to obtain more information on the topic as a whole, believing the new information from the Bible will make many of these theories impossible. If anyone is concerned we have missed something I encourage you to join me in examining the many verses in the Bible dealing with the rapture. Let's find so much information on this topic that we can put this 200-year debate to rest.

THE UNKNOWN RAPTURE SCRIPTURES

Before continuing I also want to state that we should not be surprised the rapture can be found in Revelation. God intended the book to be a "revelation" of end time events as the very first line in the book states.

Revelation 1:1
The revelation of Jesus Christ, which God gave him to show to his servants the things that must soon take place.

The Greek word translated "revelation" means exactly what you would expect it to mean. Something that is unknown is being revealed.

Now we must ask, "What is being revealed?" Is the revelation something brand new God had never mentioned to man, or an interpretation of something we had already heard? To answer this, I would have you consider what we have seen in Revelation 14-19. Was this information something God was telling us for the very first time, or did we find other information on these topics in earlier sections of the Bible? We did indeed find information on these chapters in earlier sections of the Bible and this gives us the answer to our question. The book of Revelation reveals the writings of the Old Testament.

Now we know where to find the answer to what is revealed in Revelation 14:14-16. Is this the rapture? Where are the details? The answer will be found in Old Testament prophecies and we will find the details there.

In a sense we will be discovering this in reverse order from the early church. The early church, particularly those of Jewish descent, had a much better understanding of Old Testament prophecies than the church of today. The book of Revelation took those prophecies and placed them in order, helping them understand the end time events. The modern church has at least a partial understanding of the book of Revelation but almost no knowledge of Old Testament prophecies. We have the events in order from Revelation but now need to learn the details of those events from the Old Testament.

PURPOSING A RAPTURE LOCATION

With that said, proving each of the four sections of our rapture defining scriptures, listed in our table, is fulfilled in Revelation 14:14-16 will not be our only accomplishment. We will start discovering many details from Old Testament prophecy as to how the rapture occurs. I believe much of this is almost entirely unknown.

7

The Sign of the Son of Man

We have found a portion of Revelation that has many similarities to our rapture defining scriptures. Here is that section of scripture once again.

Revelation 14:14-16
14 Then I looked, and behold, a white cloud, and seated on the cloud one like a son of man, with a golden crown on his head, and a sharp sickle in his hand. 15 And another angel came out of the temple, calling with a loud voice to him who sat on the cloud, "Put in your sickle, and reap, for the hour to reap has come, for the harvest of the earth is fully ripe." 16 So he who sat on the cloud swung his sickle across the earth, and the earth was reaped.

    We have already proven this above verse occurs on the day of the rapture, but is the verse the rapture itself? We need to examine the details of this verse and compare them with the details of our two rapture defining scriptures to find the truth on this issue.
    We will compare four sections of these scriptures as shown in the table in chapter 6. These four are the following:

THE SIGN OF THE SON OF MAN

1. The sign of the son of man.
2. The voice of the archangel.
3. The trumpet call.
4. The saints are "caught up" (rapture).

Once we prove the four items on this list are speaking of an identical event in all three passages of our table, we will know that Revelation 14:14-16 is the rapture. As a bonus, we will find numerous details about the rapture throughout this study.

Our first point of study will be to examine the sign of the son of man in this chapter. This is a phrase referenced in our rapture defining scripture in Matthew. You can see it in the table below. This phrase is very similar to the "one like a son of man" mentioned in Revelation 14:14, also shown in the table. We will prove both of these phrases are pointing to the same people and will also prove these people are mentioned in our rapture defining scripture in 1 Thessalonians as well.

	1 Thessalonians 4:13-17 (Rapture Defining Scripture)	Matthew 24:30-31 (Rapture Defining Scripture)	Revelation 14:14-16 (Purposed Rapture Location in Revelation)
Sign of the son of man	[13] But we do not want you to be uninformed, brothers, about those who are asleep, that you may not grieve as others do who have no hope. [14] For since we believe that Jesus died and rose again, even so, through Jesus, God will bring with him those who have fallen asleep. [15] For this we declare to you by a word from the Lord, that we who are alive, who are left until the coming of the Lord, will not precede those who have fallen asleep.	[30] Then will appear in heaven the sign of the Son of Man, and then all the tribes of the earth will mourn, and they will see the Son of Man coming on the clouds of heaven with power and great glory.	[14] Then I looked, and behold, a white cloud, and seated on the cloud one like a son of man, with a golden crown on his head, and a sharp sickle in his hand.

In the three verses listed in the table for the sign of the son of man we see three instances where what could be a person or persons is mentioned. Here is specifically what I am referring to.

1 Thessalonians 4:13-15   Jesus returning with the dead
Matthew 24:30   The sign of the son of man
Revelation 14:14   One like a son of man

We will examine all of these to see that they are speaking of the same thing. Two of these three verses refer to the son of man so let's begin by looking at these verses.

The Sign of the Son of Man (Matthew 24:30)

Here is Matthew's description of the sign of the Son of Man directly from part of our rapture defining scripture.

Matthew 24:30
30 Then will appear in heaven the sign of the Son of Man, and then all the tribes of the earth will mourn, and they will see the Son of Man coming on the clouds of heaven with power and great glory.

Notice this verse does not say the Son of Man will be seen but the "<u>sign</u> of the Son of Man". Examining who or what this sign is will take some time but showing what this sign is pointing to is very easy. This is actually the answer to a question the disciples asked Jesus earlier in the chapter.

Matthew 24:3
3 As he sat on the Mount of Olives, the disciples came to him privately, saying, "Tell us, when will these things be, and <u>what will be the sign of your coming and of the end of the age?</u>"

THE SIGN OF THE SON OF MAN

Jesus proceeded to tell them a bunch of events which must happen before His coming, and then finally gives the sign the disciples asked about.

Matthew 24:30a
30 Then will appear in heaven the sign of the Son of Man

So, Jesus answers the question, "What will be the sign of your coming?" by telling them it is the sign of the son of man. This sign is telling the world that Jesus' return is at hand.

We now know the event the sign is proclaiming, but what is the sign itself? We will see that it is Jesus and the church, and we will prove this in the rest of this chapter. We will look at two instances where Jesus and the church are called a sign. The second instance will also show that the church is called a sign on the day of Jesus' return.

First Instance Jesus and the Church are Called a Sign

In this first instance we will only show that Jesus and the church are referred to as a sign without referencing anything about the time of the rapture. To start this proof let's read the following passage which quotes several Old Testament scriptures, interpreting them to be Jesus speaking of the church. We will be investigating the underlined reference.

Hebrews 2:10-14
10 For it was fitting that he, for whom and by whom all things exist, in bringing many sons to glory, should make the founder of their salvation perfect through suffering. 11 For he who sanctifies and those who are sanctified all have one source. That is why he is not ashamed to call them brothers, 12 saying, "I will tell of your name to my brothers; in the midst of the congregation I will sing your praise." 13 And again, "I will put my trust in him." And again, <u>"Behold, I and the children God has given me."</u> 14 Since therefore the children share in flesh and blood, he himself likewise partook of the same things, that

through death he might destroy the one who has the power of death, that is, the devil,

The underlined section of the passage above is a reference to the book of Isaiah. Let's examine what Jesus is saying about himself and the church in Isaiah's prophecy.

Isaiah 8:18
¹⁸ <u>Behold, I and the children whom the LORD has given me are signs and portents</u> in Israel from the LORD of hosts, who dwells on Mount Zion.

We can clearly see that Jesus refers to himself and the church as a sign. This shows that the church is indeed referred to as a "sign" in scripture.

Second Instance Jesus and the Church are Called a Sign

In our first proof we only showed that the Bible does indeed refer to the church as a sign. In this second proof we will show that the church is referred to as a sign on the day of Jesus' return. This is a longer proof, but I believe the extra details will make it more convincing. To accomplish this proof, we are going interpret a prophecy in the book of Zechariah. Here is the setting where the prophecy will be made.

Zechariah 3:1-7
Then he showed me Joshua the high priest standing before the angel of the LORD, and Satan standing at his right hand to accuse him. ² And the LORD said to Satan, "The LORD rebuke you, O Satan! The LORD who has chosen Jerusalem rebuke you! Is not this a brand plucked from the fire?" ³ Now Joshua was standing before the angel, clothed with filthy garments. ⁴ And the angel said to those who were standing before him, "Remove the filthy garments from him." And to him he said, "Behold, I have taken your iniquity away from you, and I will clothe you with pure vestments." ⁵ And I said, "Let them put a

clean turban on his head." So they put a clean turban on his head and clothed him with garments. And the angel of the LORD was standing by. ⁶ *And the angel of the LORD solemnly assured Joshua,* ⁷ *"Thus says the LORD of hosts: If you will walk in my ways and keep my charge, then you shall rule my house and have charge of my courts, and I will give you the right of access among those who are standing here.*

We see that Joshua, Israel's high priest at that time, is in heaven in this vision and is standing before the Angel of the Lord. Joshua has been purified and the Lord of Hosts has begun speaking to him. The next three verses contain the prophecy we will interpret to find the sign of the son of man.

Zechariah 3:8-10
⁸ Hear now, O Joshua the high priest, you and your friends who sit before you, for they are men who are a sign: behold, I will bring my servant the Branch. ⁹ For behold, on the stone that I have set before Joshua, on a single stone with seven eyes, I will engrave its inscription, declares the LORD of hosts, and I will remove the iniquity of this land in a single day. ¹⁰ In that day, declares the LORD of hosts, every one of you will invite his neighbor to come under his vine and under his fig tree."

We see in the preceding verses that Joshua and his friends are referred to as a sign. We will prove that this represents the church being a sign on the day of the rapture by answering three questions about this prophecy.

1. Who is "the Branch"?
2. Who is giving this prophecy about "my servant the branch"?
3. When will this prophecy occur?

Once we answer these three questions we will see that the sign of the son of man is the church.

THE UNKNOWN RAPTURE SCRIPTURES

1. Who is "the Branch"?

This prophecy about "the branch" is given to Joshua and his friends. Let's look at another prophecy which mentions this same Joshua and also mentions "the branch" to help interpret this.

Zechariah 6:9-13
*⁹ And the word of the L*ORD *came to me: ¹⁰ "Take from the exiles Heldai, Tobijah, and Jedaiah, who have arrived from Babylon, and go the same day to the house of Josiah, the son of Zephaniah. ¹¹ Take from them silver and gold, and make a crown, and set it on the head of <u>Joshua, the son of Jehozadak, the high priest.</u> ¹² And say to him, 'Thus says the L*ORD *of hosts, <u>"Behold, the man whose name is the Branch</u>: for he shall branch out from his place, and he shall build the temple of the L*ORD*. ¹³ It is he who shall build the temple of the L*ORD *and shall bear royal honor, and shall sit and rule on his throne. And there shall be a priest on his throne, and the counsel of peace shall be between them both."' ¹⁴ And the crown shall be in the temple of the L*ORD *as a reminder to Helem, Tobijah, Jedaiah, and Hen the son of Zephaniah.*

Let's list our discoveries about Joshua and "the branch":
1. Joshua is referred to as "the Branch" (verse 12).
2. Joshua the High Priest is referred to as both king and priest in his role as the Branch (verse 13).

With this in mind let's look back at Zechariah 3.

Zechariah 3:8
⁸ Hear now, O Joshua the high priest, you and your friends who sit before you, for they are men who are a sign: behold, I will bring my servant the Branch.

We see that the Lord of Hosts is not only speaking to Joshua but also to his friends seated before him. They are told that the Lord of Hosts will bring His servant the Branch. Who is "the Branch"? We know from Zechariah 6:12 that Joshua is called the Branch. Remember that Joshua is prophetically both king and priest in his capacity as "The Branch". At the time this was written no one was able to be both king and priest. All kings came from the tribe of Judah, and all priests from the tribe of Levi, so there was no overlap. Therefore, this was a prophecy for the future. So, the Branch is the designation for those who are both king and priest and, in this case, that represents Joshua and his friends.

Who are these friends of Joshua who are also referred to as "the Branch" and are also both kings and priests? In the Bible the group of people referred to as being both kings and priests are the church. Here are a couple of verses which make this point.

Revelation 1:6 (KJV)
[4] John <u>to the seven churches</u> which are in Asia: Grace be unto you, and peace, from him which is, and which was, and which is to come; and from the seven Spirits which are before his throne; [5] And from Jesus Christ, who is the faithful witness, and the first begotten of the dead, and the prince of the kings of the earth. Unto him that loved us, and washed us from our sins in his own blood,[6] And hath <u>made us kings and priests</u> unto God and his Father; to him be glory and dominion for ever and ever. Amen.

1 Peter 2:9
[9] But you are a chosen race, <u>a royal priesthood</u>, a holy nation, a people for his own possession, that you may proclaim the excellencies of him who called you out of darkness into his marvelous light.

From this we know that Joshua the high priest and his friends are a prophetic reference to the church. This gives us our answer to our first question, "Who is the Branch". This will be further proven in our answer to question 2.

2. Who is giving this prophecy about "my servant the branch"?

We now know "the Branch" is the church, and Jesus referred to the church as branches in the New Testament.

John 15:5
5 I am the vine; you are the branches. Whoever abides in me and I in him, he it is that bears much fruit, for apart from me you can do nothing.

Is this the same branch referenced in both Zechariah 3 and Zechariah 6? We will see that it is the same. Notice in Zechariah 3 that the speaker refers to the Branch as His servant.

Zechariah 3:8
8 Hear now, O Joshua the high priest, you and your friends who sit before you, for they are men who are a sign: behold, I will bring <u>my servant the Branch.</u>

In John 15, later in the chapter in which Jesus refers to himself as the vine and the church as the branches, Jesus also references the Branch as His servant but makes a change to this designation.

John 15:15-16
<u>15 No longer do I call you servants, for the servant does not know what his master is doing; but I have called you friends,</u> for all that I have heard from my Father I have made known to you. 16 You did not choose me, but I chose you and appointed you that you should go and bear fruit and that your fruit should abide, so that whatever you ask the Father in my name, he may give it to you.

This helps confirm that "the Branch" from Zechariah 3:8 is also referencing the church. Since Jesus states, "no longer do I call you servants", we know that He is the Lord of Hosts who is speaking in Zechariah 3.

THE SIGN OF THE SON OF MAN

3. When will this prophecy occur?
When does this prophecy Jesus speaks over the church occur? We are given a clue in verse 10 below.

Zechariah 3:8-10
⁸ Hear now, O Joshua the high priest, you and your friends who sit before you, for they are men who are a sign: behold, I will bring my servant the Branch. ⁹ For behold, on the stone that I have set before Joshua, on a single stone with seven eyes, I will engrave its inscription, declares the LORD of hosts, and I will remove the iniquity of this land in a single day. <u>¹⁰ In that day, declares the LORD of hosts, every one of you will invite his neighbor to come under his vine and under his fig tree.</u>"

If you do a Bible search with the words "come under vine and fig tree", you will see that this phrase is a general reference describing a time of peace. However, prophetically it references a specific day which is also mentioned in an earlier prophecy from the prophet Micah.

Micah 4:1-4
It shall come to pass in the latter days that the mountain of the house of the LORD shall be established as the highest of the mountains, and it shall be lifted up above the hills; and peoples shall flow to it, ² and many nations shall come, and say: "Come, let us go up to the mountain of the LORD, to the house of the God of Jacob, that he may teach us his ways and that we may walk in his paths." For out of Zion shall go forth the law, and the word of the LORD from Jerusalem.³ He shall judge between many peoples, and shall decide disputes for strong nations far away; and they shall beat their swords into plowshares, and their spears into pruning hooks; nation shall not lift up sword against nation, neither shall they learn war anymore; ⁴ but <u>they shall sit every man under his vine and under his fig tree</u>, and no one shall make them afraid, for the mouth of the LORD of hosts has spoken.

THE UNKNOWN RAPTURE SCRIPTURES

In this verse Jesus is already ruling the world, and we know the start of Jesus' reign is the day of His return, meaning the day of the Lord. Through this prophecy mentioning *"they shall sit every man under his vine and under his fig tree"*, we know that the day referenced by Zechariah 3:8-10 is the day of Jesus' return. To further confirm this, let's look one verse back at verse 9.

Zechariah 3:9
⁹ For behold, on the stone that I have set before Joshua, on a single stone with seven eyes, I will engrave its inscription, declares the LORD of hosts, and <u>I will remove the iniquity of this land in a single day.</u>

Recall that we have already proven earlier in this book that the seven bowls of God's wrath, on the day of the Lord (the day of the rapture), will remove the sin of the world in a single day. This is further confirmation this prophecy occurs on the day of Jesus' return.

Let's list the answers to our three questions about the prophecy in Zechariah 3:8-10.
- Q1: Who is "the Branch"?
- A: Joshua and his friends are the branch, and these represent the church.
- Q2: Who is giving this prophecy about "my servant the branch"?
- A: The Lord of Hosts is giving the prophecy. The Lord of Hosts is Jesus.
- Q3: When will this prophecy occur?
- A: This prophecy occurs on the day of Jesus' return meaning the day of the Lord (rapture).

Now to tie this into the church being a sign. Let's once again examine Joshua and his friends who we know represent the church.

THE SIGN OF THE SON OF MAN

Zechariah 3:8
8 Hear now, O Joshua the high priest, you and your friends who sit before you, for <u>they are men who are a sign</u>: behold, I will bring my servant the Branch.

Joshua and his friends, representing the church, are referred to as "men who are a sign". We also know this prophecy refers to the day of the rapture. Because of these two facts we know the church is referred to as a sign on the day of Jesus' return. The sign of the Son of Man is the church. Jesus is included in this designation as he is the head of the church, the vine to the branches.

One Like a Son of Man (Revelation 14:14)

We have seen that the "sign of the son of man" is Jesus and the church. Knowing this, we can now investigate the "one like a son of man", from Revelation, to see if it relates.

Revelation 14:14
*14 Then I looked, and behold, <u>a white cloud, and seated on the cloud **one like a son of man**</u>, with a golden crown on his head, and a sharp sickle in his hand.*

How do we find the identity of this "one like a son of man" coming on the clouds? To get our answer we need to go back to the book of Daniel where this person is also mentioned and is also coming on the clouds.

Daniel 7:13-14
*13 "I saw in the night visions, and behold, <u>with the clouds of heaven there came **one like a son of man**,</u> and he came to the Ancient of Days and was presented before him. 14 And to him was given dominion and glory and a kingdom, that all peoples, nations, and languages should serve him; his dominion is an*

everlasting dominion, which shall not pass away, and his kingdom one that shall not be destroyed.

We see in the verse above this "one like a son of man", and just as in Matthew 24 he is coming on the clouds. This one like a son of man is *"given dominion and glory and a kingdom, that all peoples, nations, and languages should serve him"*. In the interpretation of this vision Daniel was told three times who is given this authority. We can use this to determine the identity of the "one like a son of man". We are told three times in the interpretation it is the saints (see the three underlined sections below).

Daniel 7:15-28
15 "As for me, Daniel, my spirit within me was anxious, and the visions of my head alarmed me. 16 I approached one of those who stood there and asked him the truth concerning all this. So he told me and made known to me the interpretation of the things. 17 'These four great beasts are four kings who shall arise out of the earth. 18 <u>But the saints of the Most High shall receive the kingdom and possess the kingdom forever, forever and ever.</u>' 19 "Then I desired to know the truth about the fourth beast, which was different from all the rest, exceedingly terrifying, with its teeth of iron and claws of bronze, and which devoured and broke in pieces and stamped what was left with its feet, 20 and about the ten horns that were on its head, and the other horn that came up and before which three of them fell, the horn that had eyes and a mouth that spoke great things, and that seemed greater than its companions. 21 As I looked, this horn made war with the saints and prevailed over them, 22 until the Ancient of Days came, and <u>judgment was given for the saints of the Most High, and the time came when the saints possessed the kingdom.</u>
23 "Thus he said: 'As for the fourth beast, there shall be a fourth kingdom on earth, which shall be different from all the kingdoms, and it shall devour the whole earth, and trample it down, and break it to pieces. 24 As for the ten horns, out of

this kingdom ten kings shall arise, and another shall arise after them; he shall be different from the former ones, and shall put down three kings. 25 He shall speak words against the Most High, and shall wear out the saints of the Most High, and shall think to change the times and the law; and they shall be given into his hand for a time, times, and half a time. 26 But the court shall sit in judgment, and his dominion shall be taken away, to be consumed and destroyed to the end. 27 <u>And the kingdom and the dominion and the greatness of the kingdoms under the whole heaven shall be given to the people of the saints of the Most High; his kingdom shall be an everlasting kingdom, and all dominions shall serve and obey him.</u>' 28 "Here is the end of the matter. As for me, Daniel, my thoughts greatly alarmed me, and my color changed, but I kept the matter in my heart."

We have seen three times that the saints will receive the kingdom. The saints must be the "one like a Son of Man" coming on the clouds since the "one like a Son of Man" receives the kingdom in the vision. We can show that the "saints" mentioned in Daniel 7 above are the church by looking at the next verse. In Daniel 7 the saints are given authority over the nations, and in Revelation 2 we are told the church will receive authority over the nations.

Revelation 2:26-29
*26 The one who conquers and who keeps my works until the end, to him <u>I will give authority over the nations</u>, 27 and he will rule them with a rod of iron, as when earthen pots are broken in pieces, even as I myself have received authority from my Father. 28 And I will give him the morning star. 29 He who has an ear, let him hear <u>what the Spirit says to the</u> **<u>churches</u>**.'*

We can see that the "one like a son of man" refers to the church. The church, along with the head of the church, Jesus, receive the kingdom.

In both Daniel 7:13-14 and Revelation 14:14 we have seen one described as one like a son of man coming on the clouds. We have proven the reference in Daniel is referring to the church. Since both verses are describe the person identically, it is no stretch to say that the one like a son of man, coming on the clouds, in Revelation 14:14 is also the church.

The Sign of the Son of Man (1 Thessalonians 4:13-15)

We have had two instances where the son of man has been used to reference Jesus and the church. Once as the sign of the son of man and another time as the one like a son of man. In our third verse relating to the rapture we see no mention of the son of man, but we are told directly of Jesus' and the churches return.

1 Thessalonians 4:13-15
13 But we do not want you to be uninformed, brothers, about those who are asleep, that you may not grieve as others do who have no hope. 14 For since we believe that Jesus died and rose again, even so, through Jesus, God will bring with him those who have fallen asleep. 15 For this we declare to you by a word from the Lord, that we who are alive, who are left until the coming of the Lord, will not precede those who have fallen asleep.

We have now seen in all three verses that the sign of the son of man, which points to Jesus' return, is Jesus and the church.

We have proven all three of our verses in the first row of the table are speaking of Jesus and the church. Revelation 14:14-16 has passed its first test to be the location of the rapture in Revelation.

8

The Voice of the Archangel

We have studied the first row of our table, the sign of the son of man, and have seen that this sign is Jesus and the church at the time of Jesus' return. Since the "one like a son of man" represented the church, Revelation 14:14-16 passed the first test toward being the location of the rapture. Now we move onto the next row of our table which deals with the voice of the archangel.

	1 Thessalonians 4:13-17 (Rapture Defining Scripture)	Matthew 24:30-31 (Rapture Defining Scripture)	Revelation 14:14-16 (Purposed Rapture Location in Revelation)
Voice of the archangel	[16] For the Lord himself will descend from heaven with a cry of command, with the voice of an archangel,	(not given)	[15] And another angel came out of the temple, calling with a loud voice to him who sat on the cloud, "Put in your sickle, and reap, for the hour to reap has come, for the harvest of the earth is fully ripe."

Our two rapture defining scriptures tell us almost nothing about the voice of the archangel. Matthew 24:30-31 tells us nothing at all, and 1 Thessalonians 4:13-17 only mentions that the archangel speaks but tells us nothing more. We obviously have some work ahead of us if we are to prove our purposed rapture location in Revelation is truly telling us the archangel's words at the time of the rapture. Here are those words.

Revelation 14:15
15 And another angel came out of the temple, calling with a loud voice to him who sat on the cloud, "<u>Put in your sickle, and reap, for the hour to reap has come, for the harvest of the earth is fully ripe.</u>"

The angel is speaking to the "one like a son of man", which we have proven is the church. To prove the harvest the angel mentions occurs at the rapture we will have to prove:
 1. The Bible speaks of a harvest for the entire church.
 2. The harvest for the church occurs at the time of the rapture.

Before we can begin to prove these two things, we will need to gather more information about the rapture from an Old Testament prophecy. We will find this information in the book of Ezekiel.

The Rapture from Ezekiel

We need to seek information about the rapture from another section of scripture to gain the knowledge we need to understand the harvest commanded through the voice of the archangel. This prophecy will give us more details relating to the rapture, and we will be able to tie it directly to one of our rapture defining scriptures. The fourteen verses we are about to read may be the most detailed section in the entire Bible related to the rapture.

THE VOICE OF THE ARCHANGEL

Ezekiel 37:1-14

The hand of the LORD was upon me, and he brought me out in the Spirit of the LORD and set me down in the middle of the valley; it was full of bones. ² And he led me around among them, and behold, there were very many on the surface of the valley, and behold, they were very dry. ³ And he said to me, "Son of man, can these bones live?" And I answered, "O Lord GOD, you know." ⁴ Then he said to me, "Prophesy over these bones, and say to them, O dry bones, hear the word of the LORD. ⁵ Thus says the Lord GOD to these bones: Behold, I will cause breath to enter you, and you shall live. ⁶ And I will lay sinews upon you, and will cause flesh to come upon you, and cover you with skin, and put breath in you, and you shall live, and you shall know that I am the LORD." ⁷ So I prophesied as I was commanded. And as I prophesied, there was a sound, and behold, a rattling, and the bones came together, bone to its bone. ⁸ And I looked, and behold, there were sinews on them, and flesh had come upon them, and skin had covered them. But there was no breath in them. ⁹ Then he said to me, "Prophesy to the breath; prophesy, son of man, and say to the breath, Thus says the Lord GOD: Come from the four winds, O breath, and breathe on these slain, that they may live." ¹⁰ So I prophesied as he commanded me, and the breath came into them, and they lived and stood on their feet, an exceedingly great army. ¹¹ Then he said to me, "Son of man, these bones are the whole house of Israel. Behold, they say, 'Our bones are dried up, and our hope is lost; we are indeed cut off.' ¹² Therefore prophesy, and say to them, Thus says the Lord GOD: Behold, I will open your graves and raise you from your graves, O my people. And I will bring you into the land of Israel. ¹³ And you shall know that I am the LORD, when I open your graves, and raise you from your graves, O my people. ¹⁴ And I will put my Spirit within you, and you shall live, and I will place you in your own land. Then you shall know that I am the LORD; I have spoken, and I will do it, declares the LORD."

THE UNKNOWN RAPTURE SCRIPTURES

We will prove that this passage is speaking of the church, and that the resurrection stated occurs at the time of the rapture. After we do this we will have the information we need to understand the harvest with the sickle, mentioned by the voice of the archangel, in Revelation 14:15. We will prove this section of scripture is speaking of the resurrection of the church in three ways. The first two proofs will show this scripture is speaking of the church and our third proof will tie this section of scripture to the time of the rapture.

Here are the three verses we will use, from Ezekiel 37, to show this chapter is speaking of the church.
1. The reference to the Holy Spirit being within the resurrected (Ezekiel 37:14).
2. The whole house of Israel reference (Ezekiel 37:11).
3. The breath that comes from the four winds (Ezekiel 37:9).

1. First Proof Ezekiel 37:1-14 is speaking of the church's resurrection. The reference to the Holy Spirit being within the resurrected (Ezekiel 37:14).

Here is the first section of this prophecy we will use to show Ezekiel 37 is speaking of the churches resurrection.

Ezekiel 37:13-14
13 And you shall know that I am the LORD, when I open your graves, and raise you from your graves, O my people. 14 And I will put my Spirit within you, and you shall live, and I will place you in your own land. Then you shall know that I am the LORD; I have spoken, and I will do it, declares the LORD."

The fact that the Holy Spirit is within the resurrected is significant. Notice in the next verse that you cannot be in the church without having the Holy Spirit within you. Also, notice that we are told the Holy Spirit will resurrect the mortal bodies of the church.

Romans 8:9-11
⁹ You, however, are not in the flesh but in the Spirit, if in fact the Spirit of God dwells in you. <u>Anyone who does not have the Spirit of Christ does not belong to him.</u> ¹⁰ But if Christ is in you, although the body is dead because of sin, the Spirit is life because of righteousness. ¹¹ <u>If the Spirit of him who raised Jesus from the dead dwells in you, he who raised Christ Jesus from the dead will also give life to your mortal bodies through his Spirit who dwells in you.</u>

We can see from this verse that all who belong to Christ, meaning the church, have the Holy Spirit within them. If you do not have the Holy Spirit within you then you have no part in Christ, meaning you are not part of the church.

We are also told the Holy Spirit raised Jesus from the dead and will raise the church from the dead in the future. In fact, the Holy Spirit is the churches guarantee or down payment on their inheritance as stated below.

Ephesians 1:13-14
¹³ In him you also, when you heard the word of truth, the gospel of your salvation, and believed in him, were sealed with the promised Holy Spirit, ¹⁴ who is the guarantee of our inheritance until we acquire possession of it, to the praise of his glory.

This inheritance cannot be received before the resurrecttion. The next verse makes this clear.

1 Corinthians 15:50-53
⁵⁰ I tell you this, brothers: <u>flesh and blood cannot inherit the kingdom of God</u>, nor does the perishable inherit the imperishable. ⁵¹ Behold! I tell you a mystery. We shall not all sleep, but we shall all be changed, ⁵² in a moment, in the

twinkling of an eye, at the last trumpet. For the trumpet will sound, and the dead will be raised imperishable, and we shall be changed. ⁵³ For this perishable body must put on the imperishable, and this mortal body must put on immortality.

Let's put together everything in this section:
1. The Holy Spirit is only within the church.
2. The Holy Spirit will raise the church from the dead just as He raised Jesus from the dead.
3. The Holy Spirit within the church is the church's guarantee to their inheritance.
4. The church's inheritance cannot be received until the Holy Spirit resurrects the church.

From this we can conclude that if the Holy Spirit is within the resurrected, in Ezekiel 37:13-14, then the resurrected must be the church.

2. Second Proof Ezekiel 37:1-14 is speaking of the church's resurrection. The whole house of Israel reference (Ezekiel 37:11)

Here is the second section of this prophecy we will use to show Ezekiel 37:1-14 is speaking of the churches resurrection.

Ezekiel 37:11-12
¹¹ Then he said to me, "Son of man, <u>these bones are the whole house of Israel</u>. Behold, they say, 'Our bones are dried up, and our hope is lost; we are indeed cut off.' ¹² Therefore prophesy, and say to them, Thus says the Lord GOD: Behold, I will open your graves and raise you from your graves, O my people. And I will bring you into the land of Israel.

Those resurrected are called the whole house of Israel. What does this mean? To get our answer let's go to the New Testament to define Israel.

THE VOICE OF THE ARCHANGEL

Romans 9:4-8
⁴ They are Israelites, and to them belong the adoption, the glory, the covenants, the giving of the law, the worship, and the promises. ⁵ To them belong the patriarchs, and from their race, according to the flesh, is the Christ, who is God over all, blessed forever. Amen. ⁶ But it is not as though the word of God has failed. For <u>not all who are descended from Israel belong to Israel</u>, ⁷ <u>and not all are children of Abraham because they are his offspring</u>, but "Through Isaac shall your offspring be named." ⁸ This means that it is not the children of the flesh who are the children of God, but the children of the promise are counted as offspring.

We can see that God does not consider anyone to be a descendant of Israel or a child of Abraham through only natural birth. Verse 6 tells us directly that not all who are descended from Israel belong to Israel. Let's focus on Abraham's descendants and see how they are defined.

Galatians 3:16
¹⁶ Now the promises were made to Abraham and to his offspring. It does not say, "And to offsprings," referring to many, but referring to one, "And to your offspring," who is Christ.

God made promises to Abraham and his offspring (singular). This offspring is Christ. We are told what this means for the church later in the chapter.

Galatians 3:29
²⁹ And if you are Christ's, then you are Abraham's offspring, heirs according to promise.

Let's follow the logic of the last three verses as they relate to Abraham and his offspring.

1. Abraham's children do not come exclusively through natural descent (Romans 9:7).
2. The promises were made to Abraham's offspring (singular) who is Christ (Galatians 3:6).
3. The church is included in Christ, meaning the church is Abraham's offspring (Galatians 3:29)

As you can see the church is Abraham's offspring. The church has been adopted into Christ becoming this offspring. The natural descendants of Abraham are only considered his offspring if they become part of Christ, meaning they join the church.

God defines Israel in the same way as Abraham's offspring. In the Old Testament those of Israel from natural descent were circumcised. In the New Testament this practice was no longer necessary, and the natural descent became inconsequential. Paul speaks of this in the verse below telling us it is the practice of the Israel of God.

Galatians 6:15-16
15 For neither circumcision counts for anything, nor uncircumcision, but a new creation. 16 And as for all who walk by this rule, peace and mercy be upon them, and upon the <u>Israel of God</u>.

This "Israel of God" is God's definition of Israel which we have already seen from Romans 9. Romans 11:1-24 goes into much greater detail describing who is in the Israel of God. In Romans 11:1-24 Israel is referred to as an olive tree. Those who believe in Jesus are grafted into the tree becoming part of Israel, and those in unbelief are cut off from the tree losing their place in Israel. Because of this, the only ones in this Israel olive tree are those who believe in Christ, meaning the church. The whole house of Israel, who will be resurrected, are the church.

3. Third Proof Ezekiel 37:1-14 is speaking of the church's resurrection. The breath that comes from the four winds (Ezekiel 37:9).

Here is our final proof that Ezekiel 37 is referring to the church's resurrection. This final proof will also show that this resurrection occurs at the time of the rapture. We will be able to directly link this passage to one of our rapture defining scriptures.

Ezekiel 37:7-9
7 So I prophesied as I was commanded. And as I prophesied, there was a sound, and behold, a rattling, and the bones came together, bone to its bone. 8 And I looked, and behold, there were sinews on them, and flesh had come upon them, and skin had covered them. But there was no breath in them 9 Then he said to me, "Prophesy to the breath; prophesy, son of man, and say to the breath, Thus says the Lord GOD: <u>*Come from the four winds*</u>*,* <u>*O breath, and breathe on these slain, that they may live.*</u>*"*

In this passage Ezekiel prophesies to the bones of many people who had been dead for a long time. When Ezekiel prophesized as commanded the bones came together, and the bodies which had turned to dust were restored and made whole. The bodies literally rose out of the ground. They were restored except that there was no breath in them. The word translated breath in this case is the exact same word for spirit. These bodies which had been restored had no spirit inside of them. Bodies cannot exist without a spirit within them as the next verse tells us.

James 2:26
26 For as the body apart from the spirit is dead, so also faith apart from works is dead.

THE UNKNOWN RAPTURE SCRIPTURES

Ezekiel is next commanded to prophesize to the breath (spirits) from the four winds of heaven to enter these bodies, so they will live. Whose spirits are these? This is actually a very easy question to answer and here is that answer directly from one of our rapture defining scriptures.

Matthew 24:30-31
*30 Then will appear in heaven the sign of the Son of Man, and then all the tribes of the earth will mourn, and they will see the Son of Man coming on the clouds of heaven with power and great glory. 31 And he will send out his angels with a loud trumpet call, and <u>they will gather his elect from the **four winds**, from one end of heaven to the other.</u>*

The spirits coming from the four winds of heaven are the spirits of "his elect". This of course means Jesus' elect. Who are Jesus' elect.

Romans 11:6-7
6 But if it is by grace, it is no longer on the basis of works; otherwise grace would no longer be grace. 7 What then? Israel failed to obtain what it was seeking. The elect obtained it, but the rest were hardened,

From this verse it is clear that the elect are the church. This gathering includes those believers still living on the earth as Mark's version of this verse makes clear.

Mark 13:26-27
*26 And then they will see the Son of Man coming in clouds with great power and glory. 27 And then he will send out the angels and gather his <u>elect from the four winds</u>, **<u>from the ends of the earth</u>** <u>to the ends of heaven.</u>*

This proves the church is resurrected in Ezekiel 37:1-14. We have also shown this event occurs at the time of the rapture, since we linked the time of this prophecy to our rapture defining scripture in Matthew. Jesus has actually re-ferred back to Ezekiel 37:9 in his answer.

From this we know the resurrection in Ezekiel 37:1-14 is the resurrection of the church at the time of the rapture.

The Church's Harvest

We have shown that Ezekiel 37:1-14 is speaking of the resurrection of the church at the time of the rapture. The information about the rapture from Ezekiel 37 will be important in understanding church's harvest, as commanded through the voice of the archangel. We will show this event once again here as a reminder to what we are trying to interpret.

Revelation 14:15
[15] And another angel came out of the temple, calling with a loud voice to him who sat on the cloud, "Put in your sickle, and reap, for the hour to reap has come, for the harvest of the earth is fully ripe."

Let's return to the two things we need to prove to show this harvest the angel speaks of occurs at the rapture:
1. Does the Bible speak of a harvest for the entire church?
2. Does this harvest for the church occurs at the time of the rapture?

1. Does the Bible speak of a harvest for the entire church?

Many references were made by Jesus referring to sowing and harvest. As an example, here is one parable Jesus told which holds many similarities to the harvest mentioned in Revelation 14:15.

Mark 4:26-29
[26] And he said, "The kingdom of God is as if a man should scatter seed on the ground. [27] He sleeps and rises night and

day, and the seed sprouts and grows; he knows not how. ²⁸ The earth produces by itself, first the blade, then the ear, then the full grain in the ear. ²⁹ But when the grain is ripe, at once he puts in the sickle, because the harvest has come."

There are many other verses in the Bible about sowing and harvest but when referring to a church-wide harvest the Bible speaks of the church's resurrection. In the verse below, we see the language of sowing and harvest used to describe death and resurrection.

1 Corinthians 15:42-46
⁴² So is it with the resurrection of the dead. What is sown is perishable; what is raised is imperishable. ⁴³ It is sown in dishonor; it is raised in glory. It is sown in weakness; it is raised in power. ⁴⁴ <u>It is sown a natural body; it is raised a spiritual body</u>. If there is a natural body, there is also a spiritual body. ⁴⁵ Thus it is written, "The first man Adam became a living being"; the last Adam became a life-giving spirit. ⁴⁶ But it is not the spiritual that is first but the natural, and then the spiritual.

We see sowing and harvest used to describe death and resurrection in the next verse as well.

Galatians 6:8
⁸ For the one who sows to his own flesh will from the flesh reap corruption, but the one who sows to the Spirit will from the Spirit reap eternal life.

From these verses we see that the dead bodies of those in the church will later be reaped (or harvested) at the time of the resurrection. From this we can see that the Bible does indeed speak of a harvest for the entire church. This confirms that an answer for our first question does indeed exist.

2. Does this harvest for the church occurs at the time of the rapture?

We have seen that the church will receive their eternal bodies in a process of harvest. The Bible makes plain that this resurrection occurs at the time of Jesus' return. We can see this in the next verse.

1 Corinthians 15:20-23
[20] But in fact Christ has been raised from the dead, the firstfruits of those who have fallen asleep. [21] For as by a man came death, by a man has come also the resurrection of the dead. [22] For as in Adam all die, so also in Christ shall all be made alive. [23] But each in his own order: Christ the firstfruits, **_then at his coming_** *_those who belong to Christ._*

Here we see the resurrection of the dead described as a harvest once again with Christ described as the first fruits of this harvest. We are then told the harvest of the church will occur at Jesus' coming. We know that the coming of Jesus is the rapture, so the church's harvest will occur at the rapture.

The Details of the Harvest

We now know that the Bible tells of a harvest for the church and that this harvest occurs at the rapture. We also know that this harvest involves the church receiving their resurrected bodies. To understand the details of this harvest let's go back to Ezekiel 37, which we already know speaks of the rapture.

Ezekiel 37:4-8
[4] Then he said to me, "Prophesy over these bones, and say to them, O dry bones, hear the word of the LORD. [5] Thus says the Lord GOD to these bones: Behold, I will cause breath to enter you, and you shall live. [6] And I will lay sinews upon you, and will cause flesh to come upon you, and cover you with skin, and put breath in you, and you shall live, and you shall

know that I am the LORD." ⁷ So I prophesied as I was commanded. And as I prophesied, there was a sound, and behold, a rattling, and the bones came together, bone to its bone. ⁸ And I looked, and behold, there were sinews on them, and flesh had come upon them, and skin had covered them. But there was no breath in them.

Here we see the spiritual bodies of those in the church being raised. These bodies are coming out of the earth like a plant. When the physical bodies of those in the church die they return to the earth. This is the body that is sown. In the verses above we see the bodies that were sown now coming out of the earth as spiritual bodies. However, no breath (spirit) is in these spiritual bodies. In other words, the church's spiritual bodies have been raised out of the ground, but the church does not yet possess them. It is time for the harvest! The spirits of those in the church will come to their resurrected bodies and harvest them, receiving the promised resurrection. We will see this event in the next part of Ezekiel 37. Remember that the word translated "breath" is the same word translated "spirit".

Ezekiel 37:9-14
⁹ Then he said to me, <u>"Prophesy to the breath; prophesy, son of man, and say to the breath, Thus says the Lord GOD: Come from the four winds, O breath, and breathe on these slain, that they may live."</u> ¹⁰ So I prophesied as he commanded me, and the breath came into them, and they lived and stood on their feet, an exceedingly great army. ¹¹ Then he said to me, "Son of man, these bones are the whole house of Israel. Behold, they say, 'Our bones are dried up, and our hope is lost; we are indeed cut off.' ¹² Therefore prophesy, and say to them, Thus says the Lord GOD: Behold, I will open your graves and raise you from your graves, O my people. And I will bring you into the land of Israel. ¹³ And you shall know that I am the LORD, when I open your graves, and raise you from your graves, O my people. ¹⁴ And I will put my Spirit within you, and you shall

live, and I will place you in your own land. Then you shall know that I am the LORD; I have spoken, and I will do it, declares the LORD."

As a reminder, we can tie the underlined portion of the above verse directly to our rapture defining scripture in Matthew 24:30-31, meaning it occurs at the rapture.

Wherever the church's spirits are on earth or heaven, they will be brought by the angels to harvest their spiritual bodies. Is this the harvest commanded by the voice of the archangel? Let's go back to our purposed rapture location in Revelation.

Revelation 14:15
15 And another angel came out of the temple, calling with a loud voice to him who sat on the cloud, "Put in your sickle, and reap, for the hour to reap has come, for the harvest of the earth is fully ripe."

Let's examine what we know about this verse:
1. We know the angel in this verse is speaking to the church, since we proved the "one like a son of man" is the church in the last chapter.
2. The angel in this verse commands the church to go to the earth and harvest. We have seen that the church-wide harvest mentioned within the Bible refers to the resurrection.
3. We have tied this churchwide harvest, meaning the resurrection, directly to our rapture defining scripture in Matthew showing this event is the rapture.

To reiterate, if the angel is commanding a church-wide harvest this must be the resurrection of the church. Also, since this is the resurrection of the church this resurrection must take place at the rapture since the event is directly linked to our rapture defining scripture in Matthew. From all of this we can clearly see the angel in our purposed rapture location is telling the church to harvest their resurrected bodies at the time of the rapture.

Let's compare our result with the mention of the angel in our rapture defining scripture in 1 Thessalonians 4.

Revelation 14:15
15 And another angel came out of the temple, calling with a loud voice to him who sat on the cloud, "Put in your sickle, and reap, for the hour to reap has come, for the harvest of the earth is fully ripe."

We see in our purposed rapture location that the angel is giving this command to the church at the time we have shown to be the rapture. In our rapture defining scripture below, we also see an angel giving a command at a time we know to be the rapture.

1 Thessalonians 4:16
16 For the Lord himself will descend from heaven with a cry of command, with the voice of an archangel, and with the sound of the trumpet of God. And the dead in Christ will rise first.

The underlined section of this verse, perhaps better translated, "with a cry of command through the voice of an archangel", also tells of an angel giving a command at the time of the rapture. Since both verses tell of an angel giving a command at the start of the same exact event, we can have confidence that we are reading about the same angel in both passages.

Revelation 14:14-16 has passed its second test to be the location of the rapture.

9

The Trumpet Call

We have now shown that the sign of the son of man and the voice of the archangel are speaking of identical people and events in both our purposed rapture location in Revelation and our two rapture defining scriptures. Now onto the third row of our table which shows the trumpet call.

	1 Thessalonians 4:13-17 (Rapture Defining Scripture)	Matthew 24:30-31 (Rapture Defining Scripture)	Revelation 14:14-16 (Purposed Rapture Location in Revelation)
Trumpet call	and with the sound of the trumpet of God.	[31] And he will send out his angels with a loud trumpet call,	(not given)

You can see the obvious problem we will have in trying to prove the same trumpet is blown in our purposed rapture location. No mention of a trumpet is given in this verse. To prove a trumpet is blown at this point in Revelation we will need to examine the two separate harvests mentioned in Revelation 14. Both harvests are shown in the next passage.

Revelation 14:14-20

14 Then I looked, and behold, a white cloud, and seated on the cloud one like a son of man, with a golden crown on his head, and a sharp sickle in his hand. 15 And another angel came out of the temple, calling with a loud voice to him who sat on the cloud, "Put in your sickle, and reap, for the hour to reap has come, for the harvest of the earth is fully ripe." 16 So he who sat on the cloud swung his sickle across the earth, and the earth was reaped.

17 Then another angel came out of the temple in heaven, and he too had a sharp sickle. 18 And another angel came out from the altar, the angel who has authority over the fire, and he called with a loud voice to the one who had the sharp sickle, "Put in your sickle and gather the clusters from the vine of the earth, for its grapes are ripe." 19 So the angel swung his sickle across the earth and gathered the grape harvest of the earth and threw it into the great winepress of the wrath of God. 20 And the winepress was trodden outside the city, and blood flowed from the winepress, as high as a horse's bridle, for 1,600 stadia.

You can see above that each of the paragraphs refer to a different harvest. From verse 17 we see the second harvest comes immediately after the first is completed.

Revelation 14:17
17 <u>Then</u> another angel came out of the temple in heaven, and he too had a sharp sickle.

We have two harvests which occur one after the other. This presents us with an opportunity to prove the trumpet call occurs in the first harvest (our purposed rapture location), since this is not the only place in scripture these two harvests appear side by side. We will examine several sections of scripture that put these two harvests together.

THE TRUMPET CALL

	Revelation 14:14-20	Joel 2:1-2 / Joel 3:12-13	Isaiah 18:3-6
First Harvest	[14] Then I looked, and behold, a white cloud, and seated on the cloud one like a son of man, with a golden crown on his head, and a sharp sickle in his hand. [15] And another angel came out of the temple, calling with a loud voice to him who sat on the cloud, "Put in your sickle, and reap, for the hour to reap has come, for the harvest of the earth is fully ripe." [16] So he who sat on the cloud swung his sickle across the earth, and the earth was reaped.	Blow a trumpet in Zion; sound an alarm on my holy mountain! Let all the inhabitants of the land tremble, for the day of the LORD is coming; it is near, [2] a day of darkness and gloom, a day of clouds and thick darkness! Like blackness there is spread upon the mountains a great and powerful people; their like has never been before, nor will be again after them through the years of all generations.	[3] All you inhabitants of the world, you who dwell on the earth, when a signal is raised on the mountains, look! When a trumpet is blown, hear!
Second Harvest	[17] Then another angel came out of the temple in heaven, and he too had a sharp sickle. [18] And another angel came out from the altar, the angel who has authority over the fire, and he called with a loud voice to the one who had the sharp sickle, "Put in your sickle and gather the clusters from the vine of the earth, for its grapes are ripe." [19] So the angel swung his sickle across the earth and gathered the grape harvest of the earth and threw it into the great winepress of the wrath of God. [20] And the winepress was trodden outside the city, and blood flowed from the winepress, as high as a horse's bridle, for 1,600 stadia.	[12] Let the nations stir themselves up and come up to the Valley of Jehoshaphat; for there I will sit to judge all the surrounding nations. [13] Put in the sickle, for the harvest is ripe. Go in, tread, for the winepress is full. The vats overflow, for their evil is great.	[4] For thus the LORD said to me: "I will quietly look from my dwelling like clear heat in sunshine, like a cloud of dew in the heat of harvest." [5] For before the harvest, when the blossom is over, and the flower becomes a ripening grape, he cuts off the shoots with pruning hooks, and the spreading branches he lops off and clears away. [6] They shall all of them be left to the birds of prey of the mountains and to the beasts of the earth. And the birds of prey will summer on them, and all the beasts of the earth will winter on them.

The Second Harvest

We will start with the second harvest. All the verses listed below can be read in the table on the previous page. All three verses have the following four things included within them:

1. A Sickle
   - Revelation 14:17 - mentions a sickle which will be used for the grape harvest.
   - Isaiah 18:5 - Here we see a pruning hook instead of a sickle. Both are similar reaping devices and using one instead of the other does not change the meaning of the prophecy.
   - Joel 3:13 – This verse also mentions the sickle.
2. A Grape Harvest
   - Revelation 14:18 - the sickle is used to harvest the grapes.
   - Isaiah 18:5 - the pruning hook is used to harvest the grapes.
   - Joel 3:13 - the harvest from the sickle is put in the winepress, showing this is also a grape harvest.
3. Grapes are used as symbols for humans.
   - Revelation 14:20 - blood comes from the grapes showing they represent humans.
   - Isaiah 18:6 - birds of prey are attracted to the grapes signifying the presence of blood. Therefore, the grapes represent humans.
   - Joel 3:12-13 - makes clear that the nations are gathered to be harvested.
4. The humans referred to as grapes are completely destroyed.
   - Revelation 14:20 - the gigantic amount of blood mentioned shows the complete destruction of these people.
   - Isaiah 18:6 - the large amount of time it will take for the animals to eat the dead show the complete destruction.
   - Joel 3:13 - the overflowing winepress shows their destruction.

We have shown four similarities between these three passages for the second harvest. Is this enough to prove the harvest is the same in these three scriptures?

To answer this question let's first discuss why Old Testament prophecy seems confusing to many. When any part of an Old Testament prophecy is quoted, the quotation has often been kept as minimal as possible. For example, many of you have probably heard the following verse mentioned:

Hosea 4:6a
My people are destroyed for lack of knowledge;

Notice this is not even the complete sentence. The meaning of this verse completely changes when we quote the entire sentence. As I stated earlier in the book, "Many false doctrines throughout church history would likely have never existed if their creators had bothered to read the two or three verses before and after the scriptures used to justify their beliefs". Here is what the verse says when we complete the rest of the sentence.

Hosea 4:6
My people are destroyed for lack of knowledge; because you have rejected knowledge, I reject you from being a priest to me.

Reading the entire sentence completely changes the meaning. It is not the lack of studying that is causing the people to be destroyed, but the rejection of the knowledge they already have. We could expand even this even further to discover to whom "My people" is referring, and we could then expand again and again until we would see the message of the entire chapter. This is what we should be learning. The message of the entire chapter is what God was trying to convey to us. Pulling out a sentence or two and forming a belief around it is not following God. Everything needs to be put in context. We should be learning the message of this entire chapter and not the message of the half sentence.

When you learn the prophetic Old Testament in fragments the prophecies become a giant jigsaw puzzle. When you pull a single verse out of a chapter or use a half sentence you can literally make these scriptures say anything. However, these prophecies are not nearly as fragmented as many in the church believe. There are not nearly as many pieces to the puzzle as it may seem, and these pieces are usually chapter sized rather than verse sized! For example, the entire book of Joel is a single prophecy that occurs over a single day, the day of the Lord. My point is that each chapter of the prophetic Old Testament should be viewed as one or several prophecies, and not fragments of numerous prophecies.

With that said, finding multiple chapters in the Bible that mentions a sickle (pruning hook), grapes, and a harvest all together is not as common as you might believe. Just how common is it to find these three things together? If you did a search for both sickle and pruning hook you would find that only six verses in the prophetic books of the Old Testament mention either of these. The Old Testament prophetic books also mention "grape" 18 times and mention "harvest" 21 times (may differ slightly in different translations). This gives a maximum of six locations all three of these could potentially be together in the prophetic Old Testament. Now, if we expand our search to the entire Bible we would see that all three of these words are only found together in two places, Revelation 14:19 and Isaiah 18:5. The only other place sickle and harvest are together is in Joel 3:13 and in this verse the grapes are implied through the winepress. In other words, the three passages we are using are likely the only three places in the entire Bible where sickle/pruning hook, harvest, and grape are all together. Since all three of these verses have been shown to define an identical event we can be certain all are mentioning the same harvest.

The First Harvest

Let's examine the first harvest from our table once again.

	Revelation 14:14-20	Joel 2:1-2 / Joel 3:12-13	Isaiah 18:3-6
First Harvest	[14] Then I looked, and behold, a white cloud, and seated on the cloud one like a son of man, with a golden crown on his head, and a sharp sickle in his hand. [15] And another angel came out of the temple, calling with a loud voice to him who sat on the cloud, "Put in your sickle, and reap, for the hour to reap has come, for the harvest of the earth is fully ripe." [16] So he who sat on the cloud swung his sickle across the earth, and the earth was reaped.	Blow a trumpet in Zion; sound an alarm on my holy mountain! Let all the inhabitants of the land tremble, for the day of the LORD is coming; it is near, [2] a day of darkness and gloom, a day of clouds and thick darkness! Like blackness there is spread upon the mountains a great and powerful people; their like has never been before, nor will be again after them through the years of all generations.	[3] All you inhabitants of the world, you who dwell on the earth, when a signal is raised on the mountains, look! When a trumpet is blown, hear!

We have just shown that the events immediately following these three passages are identical and have named them the second harvest. We will now show these three sections of scripture are the same event as well. Once we accomplish this goal we will have proven a trumpet is blown in the first harvest in Revelation, since the two verses in the table outside of Revelation mention the trumpet.

Since we are proving Revelation 14:14-16 is the rapture we must prove the other two events are the rapture as well. We will prove this in both Joel 2:1-2 and Isaiah 18:3. We will start with Joel 2:1-2.

THE UNKNOWN RAPTURE SCRIPTURES

The Rapture from Joel 2

Could Joel 2:1-2 really be a reference to the rapture? We will take a closer look at these verses to find the truth. Let's examine this passage. We will examine it in the King James Version, since it is translated much more accurately for these verses than our standard ESV.

Joel 2:1-2 (KJV)
Blow ye the trumpet in Zion, and sound an alarm in my holy mountain: let all the inhabitants of the land tremble: for the day of the LORD cometh, for it is nigh at hand; ² A day of darkness and of gloominess, a day of clouds and of thick darkness, as the morning spread upon the mountains: a great people and a strong; there hath not been ever the like, neither shall be any more after it, even to the years of many generations.

We will examine three aspects of this passage and show the following:
1. These verses occur on the day of the rapture.
2. The trumpet blown here is blown on the day of the rapture.
3. This is the resurrection of the church.

1. These verses occur on the day of the rapture.

This section of scripture clearly occurs on the day of the Lord since the first verse of this passage mention this day.

Joel 2:1 (KJV)
Blow ye the trumpet in Zion, and sound an alarm in my holy mountain: let all the inhabitants of the land tremble: for <u>the day of the LORD</u> cometh, for it is nigh at hand;

We have already proven that the day of the Lord is the day of the rapture, so we know these verses occur on the day of the rapture.

THE TRUMPET CALL

2. The trumpet blown here is blown on the day of the rapture.
In this passage, speaking of the day of the rapture, a trumpet is blown.

Joel 2:1 (KJV)
<u>Blow ye the trumpet in Zion</u>, and sound an alarm in my holy mountain: let all the inhabitants of the land tremble: for <u>the day of the LORD</u> cometh, for it is nigh at hand;

We could not be told much more clearly that this trumpet is blown on the day of the Lord, meaning the day of the rapture.

3. This is the resurrection of the church.
The trumpet blown on the day of the rapture signals the time of the church's resurrection. We are told this below.

1 Corinthians 15:51-5
[51] Behold! I tell you a mystery. We shall not all sleep, but we shall all be changed, [52] in a moment, in the twinkling of an eye, <u>at the last trumpet. For the trumpet will sound, and the dead will be raised imperishable,</u> and we shall be changed. [53] For this perishable body must put on the imperishable, and this mortal body must put on immortality.

We can clearly see the resurrection occurs when a trumpet is blown.

Remember back to our study from Ezekiel 37. At the rapture, the resurrected bodies of those in the church will be formed out of the dust of their dead physical bodies on earth. At this time, the voice of the archangel will tell the spirits of those in the church to reap their resurrected bodies. Could Joel 2:1-2 be the time of this reaping? Examine the underlined section in the next passage.

Joel 2:1-2 (KJV)
Blow ye the trumpet in Zion, and sound an alarm in my holy mountain: let all the inhabitants of the land tremble: for the

*day of the L*ORD *cometh, for it is nigh at hand;* ² *A day of darkness and of gloominess, a day of clouds and of thick darkness,* <u>as the morning spread upon the mountains: a great people and a strong; there hath not been ever the like, neither shall be any more after it, even to the years of many generations.</u>

A group of people has appeared on the mountains after the trumpet is blown on the day of the rapture. We will see these people are the resurrected church.

Here is how we are purposing the church is resurrected in these verses. Verse two starts with a setting of great darkness. As the trumpet blows a light suddenly appears upon the mountains as the morning sun would at dawn. This light which appears on the mountains is the resurrected bodies of those in the church. The members of every generation of the church reap their resurrected bodies and get up off the ground. The church has become a people great and strong as this verse mentions. No group of people has ever been so great or strong in the past and no group will ever again reach the same level in the future.

This is what we purpose is happening in this verse and now we will prove this is true. To prove the people mentioned in this passage are the church we will compare Joel 2:1-11 with Isaiah 13:1-13. Both of these verses are listed below, and both speak of the same event.

Joel 2:1-11
*Blow a trumpet in Zion; sound an alarm on my holy mountain! Let all the inhabitants of the land tremble, for the day of the L*ORD *is coming; it is near,* ² *a day of darkness and gloom, a day of clouds and thick darkness! Like blackness there is spread upon the mountains a great and powerful people; their like has never been before, nor will be again after them through the years of all generations.* ³ *Fire devours before them, and behind them a flame burns. The land is like the garden of Eden before them, but behind them a desolate wilderness,*

THE TRUMPET CALL

and nothing escapes them. ⁴ Their appearance is like the appearance of horses, and like war horses they run. ⁵ As with the rumbling of chariots, they leap on the tops of the mountains, like the crackling of a flame of fire devouring the stubble, like a powerful army drawn up for battle. ⁶ Before them peoples are in anguish; all faces grow pale. ⁷ Like warriors they charge; like soldiers they scale the wall. They march each on his way; they do not swerve from their paths. ⁸ They do not jostle one another; each marches in his path; they burst through the weapons and are not halted. ⁹ They leap upon the city, they run upon the walls, they climb up into the houses, they enter through the windows like a thief. ¹⁰ The earth quakes before them; the heavens tremble. The sun and the moon are darkened, and the stars withdraw their shining. ¹¹ The LORD utters his voice before his army, for his camp is exceedingly great; he who executes his word is powerful. For the day of the LORD is great and very awesome; who can endure it?

Before we go on to read Isaiah 13:1-13 I need to make some points about this verse. Before now I had been using the King James Version of the Bible in showing Joel 2:1-2. This is because that version translates these verses much more accurately. Notice in verse 2 the ESV tells us darkness is spread upon the mountains while the KJV tells us morning is spread upon the mountains. This word translated both darkness and morning appears to have to do with "dawn". The ESV chose to translate this word darkness because they believed it kept the context of the first part of verse 2. However, by trying to interpret the verse while translating they made a mistake, in my opinion. When reading the Old Testament, which even scholars often do not understand, you will usually be much better off with a more literal translation. This is not to put down the other translations. As you know I am using the ESV in almost every instance. However, when trying to understand an unknown scripture I will often switch to a more literal version.

THE UNKNOWN RAPTURE SCRIPTURES

One other thing you may have noticed in the above verse is how the church is described at the resurrection. For example, in verse 4 we are told they have the appearance of horses. This appearance has to do with the angels who are with the church at the time of this event, but the study of that is beyond the scope of this book. We do not have the time at present to interpret every part of these verses, but I plan to cover all of this in later books. We are focusing on a single part of the day of the Lord, the rapture. However, this does not even cover 10% of all that happens on this day. For a more complete picture I would suggest reading the entire book of Joel and Revelation 14-19. For now, our only concern is proving this passage is speaking of the church, and we will fully accomplish that goal. With that said let's move onto Isaiah 13.

Isaiah 13:1-13
The oracle concerning Babylon which Isaiah the son of Amoz saw. ² On a bare hill raise a signal; cry aloud to them; wave the hand for them to enter the gates of the nobles. ³ I myself have commanded my consecrated ones, and have summoned my mighty men to execute my anger, my proudly exulting ones. ⁴ The sound of a tumult is on the mountains as of a great multitude! The sound of an uproar of kingdoms, of nations gathering together! The LORD of hosts is mustering a host for battle. ⁵ They come from a distant land, from the end of the heavens, the LORD and the weapons of his indignation, to destroy the whole land. ⁶ Wail, for the day of the LORD is near; as destruction from the Almighty it will come! ⁷ Therefore all hands will be feeble, and every human heart will melt. ⁸ They will be dismayed: pangs and agony will seize them; they will be in anguish like a woman in labor. They will look aghast at one another; their faces will be aflame. ⁹ Behold, the day of the LORD comes, cruel, with wrath and fierce anger, to make the land a desolation and to destroy its sinners from it. ¹⁰ For the stars of the heavens and their constellations will not give their light; the sun will be dark at its rising, and the moon will not shed its light. ¹¹ I will punish the world for its evil, and the

THE TRUMPET CALL

wicked for their iniquity; I will put an end to the pomp of the arrogant, and lay low the pompous pride of the ruthless. ^{12} *I will make people more rare than fine gold, and mankind than the gold of Ophir.* ^{13} *Therefore I will make the heavens tremble, and the earth will be shaken out of its place, at the wrath of the LORD of hosts*

Both of the preceding verses are speaking of the same event. Notice the similarities in the table below:

	Joel 2:1-11	Isaiah 13:1-13
Day of the Lord Mentioned	Verses 1, 11	Verse 6
People Appear on the Mountains	Verse 2	Verses 4, 5
The Lord's Army	Verse 4	Verse 11
Sun/Moon/Stars Darkened	Verse 10	Verse 10
Heavens and Earth Shaken	Verse 10	Verse 13

You can see from the table that these two sections of scripture are speaking of the same event on the day of the rapture. Since they are speaking of the same event we can prove the people on the mountains in Joel 2:1-11 are the church by proving the people on the mountains in Isaiah 13:1-13 are the church. We will examine two things in Isaiah 13:1-13 which show us the identity of these people.
1. The signal on the mountain
2. Those coming from the end of the heavens

THE UNKNOWN RAPTURE SCRIPTURES

1. The signal on the mountain

The first way we will show the people appearing on the mountains are the church is in verse 2.

Isaiah 13:2a
² On a bare hill raise a signal;

The word hill in the above verse is the same Hebrew word translated mountain in Joel 2:1-2. Other translations, including the King James Version, translate this word mountain. Because of this, it is no mistake to label this point the signal on the mountain.

We have clearly seen this chapter is speaking of the day of the Lord, meaning the day of the rapture. What signal is raised on this day? Recall the question Jesus' disciples asked him about the sign of His coming.

Matthew 24:3
³ As he sat on the Mount of Olives, the disciples came to him privately, saying, "Tell us, when will these things be, and <u>what will be the sign of your coming and of the end of the age?</u>"

Jesus told his disciples events which must take place before his coming and finally answered the question in verse thirty.

Matthew 24:30
³⁰ Then will appear in heaven <u>the sign of the Son of Man</u>, and then all the tribes of the earth will mourn, and they will see the Son of Man coming on the clouds of heaven with power and great glory.

We have already spent an entire chapter interpreting this sign to be the church. We can be sure that the people appearing on the mountain, who are a sign on the day of the rapture, must be the church.

THE TRUMPET CALL

2. Those coming from the end of the heavens
The second way we will show the people appearing on the mountains are the church is in verses 4-5.

Isaiah 13:4-5a
⁴ The sound of a tumult is on the mountains as of a great multitude! The sound of an uproar of kingdoms, of nations gathering together! The LORD of hosts is mustering a host for battle. ⁵ They come from a distant land, from the end of the heavens,

We are told those on the mountains come from the end of the heavens. We already know who comes from the end of the heavens on the day of the Lord from our rapture defining scripture.

Matthew 24:30-31
³⁰ Then will appear in heaven the sign of the Son of Man, and then all the tribes of the earth will mourn, and they will see the Son of Man coming on the clouds of heaven with power and great glory. ³¹ And he will send out his angels with a loud trumpet call, and they will gather his elect from the four winds, <u>from one end of heaven to the other</u>.

It is clear that those appearing on the mountains, who come from the end of the heavens, are the church. Since we have proven the people on the mountains in Isaiah 13:1-13 are the church we know the people on the mountains in Joel 2:1-11 are also the church. We have proven Joel 2:1-11 is speaking of the resurrection of the church. By combining Joel 2:1-11 and Isaiah 13:1-13 we can see that Joel 2:1-2 is the time of the rapture.

The Rapture from Isaiah 18
We have shown that Joel 2:1-2 is the rapture but what about Isaiah 18:3? Can we also prove that this short verse is the rapture?

THE UNKNOWN RAPTURE SCRIPTURES

Isaiah 18:3
³ All you inhabitants of the world, you who dwell on the earth, when a signal is raised on the mountains, look! When a trumpet is blown, hear!

We are not given much information in this verse, but this is clearly an event that occurs worldwide since it is spoken to all who dwell on the earth. Two things occur in this verse: a trumpet is blown, and a signal is raised. Due to its location immediately before the second harvest, the mention of the signal on the mountains, and the mention of the trumpet we will be able to show this is a reference to the rapture. We have just finished studying Joel 2:1-11 and Isaiah 13:1-13. These scriptures mention both the signal and the trumpet. Here Joel 2:1-2 mentions the trumpet at the rapture.

Joel 2:1-2 (KJV)
<u>Blow ye the trumpet in Zion</u>, and sound an alarm in my holy mountain: let all the inhabitants of the land tremble: for the day of the LORD cometh, for it is nigh at hand; ² A day of darkness and of gloominess, a day of clouds and of thick darkness, as the morning spread upon the mountains: a great people and a strong; there hath not been ever the like, neither shall be any more after it, even to the years of many generations.

Below, Isaiah 13:2-3 mentions the signal raised on the mountains at the time of the rapture.

Isaiah 13:2-3
² <u>On a bare hill raise a signal</u>; cry aloud to them; wave the hand for them to enter the gates of the nobles. ³ I myself have commanded my consecrated ones, and have summoned my mighty men to execute my anger, my proudly exulting ones.

Because of the signal, the trumpet, and most importantly the location of Isaiah 18:3 immediately before the second harvest, we know this verse is a reference to the rapture. With this we have shown that all three scriptures in our table for the first harvest are the same event.

Here is what we have shown which will help us prove a trumpet is blown in our purposed rapture location:
1. Both the first and second harvest are the same event in all three passages.
2. The second harvest follows closely after the first harvest in all three passages.
3. The first harvest is the day of the Lord meaning the day of the rapture.

From these three things we can be certain all three verses for the first harvest are speaking of the same harvest mentioned in Revelation 14:14-16. Since all three verses are speaking of the same event, we can combine the details of the three passages to get a more complete picture. Notice that two of the verses mention a trumpet being blown.

Joel 2:1-2
<u>Blow a trumpet in Zion</u>; sound an alarm on my holy mountain! Let all the inhabitants of the land tremble, for the day of the LORD is coming; it is near, ² a day of darkness and gloom, a day of clouds and thick darkness! Like blackness there is spread upon the mountains a great and powerful people; their like has never been before, nor will be again after them through the years of all generations.

Isaiah 18:3
³ All you inhabitants of the world, you who dwell on the earth, when a signal is raised on the mountains, look! <u>When a trumpet is blown, hear!</u>

THE UNKNOWN RAPTURE SCRIPTURES

Since we have proven both of these verses are speaking of the same harvest that occurs in our purposed rapture location in Revelation 14:14-16 we can be certain a trumpet is blown in this location as well.

Revelation 14:14-16 has passed our third test in determining if it is the location of the rapture. We now know a trumpet is blown in this event just as in our two rapture defining scriptures. Only one more test remains.

10

The Saints are "Caught Up" (Rapture)

Our final test to confirm Revelation 14:14-16 is the raptures location involves the saints being "caught up", meaning the rapture itself. This is most clearly shown in our rapture defining scripture in 1 Thessalonians 4:17.

	1 Thessalonians 4:13-17 (Rapture Defining Scripture)	Matthew 24:30-31 (Rapture Defining Scripture)	Revelation 14:14-16 (Purposed Rapture Location in Revelation)
The saints "caught up" (rapture)	And the dead in Christ will rise first. [17] Then we who are alive, who are left, will be caught up together with them in the clouds to meet the Lord in the air, and so we will always be with the Lord.	And they will gather his elect from the four winds, from one end of heaven to the other.	[16] So he who sat on the cloud swung his sickle across the earth, and the earth was reaped.

All three of our scriptures end differently:
- Revelation 14:14-16 – Ends with the church reaping their resurrected bodies.

- Matthew 24:30-31 – Ends with the resurrected bodies of the church being gathered into one place, although meeting Jesus in the air is not mentioned.
- 1 Thessalonians 4:13-17 – Ends with the resurrected bodies of the church meeting Jesus in the air.

Since none of these verses end exactly the same way, we will link our purposed rapture location to each of our rapture defining scriptures separately.

Linking Our Purposed Rapture Location to our Rapture Defining Scripture in Mathew

We have proven that the following verse from our purposed rapture location is speaking of the church harvesting their resurrected bodies on the earth.

Revelation 14:16
16 So he who sat on the cloud swung his sickle across the earth, and the earth was reaped.

Our proposed rapture location stops speaking of this event at this point before the church ascends back to the clouds to meet the Lord in the air. This ending point comes earlier than our rapture defining scripture in Matthew which adds the fact that the church is "gathered" to some location.

Matthew 24:31
31 And he will send out his angels with a loud trumpet call, and they will <u>gather</u> his elect from the four winds, from one end of heaven to the other.

It will be very easy to link these two verses together since we have already done so more than once. The answer is in Ezekiel.

THE SAINTS ARE "CAUGHT UP" (RAPTURE)

Ezekiel 37:9-10
⁹ Then he said to me, "Prophesy to the breath; prophesy, son of man, and say to the breath, Thus says the Lord GOD: <u>Come from the four winds</u>, O breath, and breathe on these slain, that they may live." ¹⁰ So I prophesied as he commanded me, and the breath came into them, and they lived and stood on their feet, an exceedingly great army.

We have already proven in an earlier chapter that this event is fulfilled in our purposed rapture location and is the resurrection of the church. We can also link the underlined section of this verse directly to our rapture defining scripture in Matthew.

Matthew 24:31
³¹ And he will send out his angels with a loud trumpet call, and they will <u>gather his elect from the four winds</u>, from one end of heaven to the other.

This effectively links together both Revelation 14:16 and Matthew 24:31. Since both occur at the resurrection of the church, we know that when the elect are gathered in our rapture defining scripture in Matthew they must also be gathered in our purposed rapture location in Revelation.

Linking our Purposed Rapture Location to our Rapture Defining Scripture in 1 Thessalonians

We have shown that at the end of our purposed rapture location in Revelation the resurrected church is gathered somewhere. Can we prove this place is in the air to meet Jesus? We can in fact do this by introducing another Old Testament scripture that links the resurrection and Jesus appearing in the air. Here is that passage.

THE UNKNOWN RAPTURE SCRIPTURES

Zechariah 9:9-17
9 Rejoice greatly, O daughter of Zion! Shout aloud, O daughter of Jerusalem! Behold, your king is coming to you; righteous and having salvation is he, humble and mounted on a donkey, on a colt, the foal of a donkey. 10 I will cut off the chariot from Ephraim and the war horse from Jerusalem; and the battle bow shall be cut off, and he shall speak peace to the nations; his rule shall be from sea to sea, and from the River to the ends of the earth. 11 As for you also, because of the blood of my covenant with you, I will set your prisoners free from the waterless pit. 12 Return to your stronghold, O prisoners of hope; today I declare that I will restore to you double. 13 For I have bent Judah as my bow; I have made Ephraim its arrow. I will stir up your sons, O Zion, against your sons, O Greece, and wield you like a warrior's sword.

14 <u>Then the LORD will appear over them</u>, and his arrow will go forth like lightning; the Lord GOD will sound the trumpet and will march forth in the whirlwinds of the south. 15 The LORD of hosts will protect them, and they shall devour, and tread down the sling stones, and they shall drink and roar as if drunk with wine, and be full like a bowl, drenched like the corners of the altar. 16 On that day the LORD their God will save them, as the flock of his people; for like the jewels of a crown they shall shine on his land. 17 For how great is his goodness, and how great his beauty! Grain shall make the young men flourish, and new wine the young women.

In the underlined section of the scripture above, we see a reference to Jesus appearing in the air. Let's begin by examining if this is really Jesus. Let's look at the first verse of this passage.

Zechariah 9:9
9 Rejoice greatly, O daughter of Zion! Shout aloud, O daughter of Jerusalem! Behold, your king is coming to you; righteous and having salvation is he, humble and mounted on a donkey, on a colt, the foal of a donkey.

THE SAINTS ARE "CAUGHT UP" (RAPTURE)

Many of you who are familiar with the Bible will likely recognize this verse, since it is quoted in the New Testament.

John 12:12-16
12 The next day the large crowd that had come to the feast heard that Jesus was coming to Jerusalem. 13 So they took branches of palm trees and went out to meet him, crying out, "Hosanna! Blessed is he who comes in the name of the Lord, even the King of Israel!" 14 And Jesus found a young donkey and sat on it, just <u>as it is written, 15 "Fear not, daughter of Zion; behold, your king is coming, sitting on a donkey's colt!"</u> 16 His disciples did not understand these things at first, but when Jesus was glorified, then they remembered that these things had been written about him and had been done to him.

This prophecy in Zechariah 9:9 was fulfilled by Jesus. This tells us that He is involved in this prophecy. He could certainly be the one who appears in the air in verse fourteen. We will find more evidence of this fact as we go along. Although Jesus fulfilled verse nine during His time on earth almost 2000 years back, he has yet to fulfill the rest of the chapter. For example, look at the very next verse.

Zechariah 9:10
10 I will cut off the chariot from Ephraim and the war horse from Jerusalem; and the battle bow shall be cut off, and he shall speak peace to the nations; his rule shall be from sea to sea, and from the River to the ends of the earth.

This has obviously not been fulfilled since Jesus is not ruling over the world. This is a common theme with the prophecies Jesus fulfilled during His earthly ministry. Jesus fulfilled parts of many prophecies during His time on earth almost 2000 years ago, but He will not fulfill the entire prophecy until His return on the day of the Lord. In other cases, he has entirely fulfilled prophecies in the past, but will fulfill them once again in the future.

Let's get back to Zechariah 9 and see what the chapter is saying about the future.

Zechariah 9:11-17
11 As for you also, because of the blood of my covenant with you, I will set your prisoners free from the waterless pit. 12 Return to your stronghold, O prisoners of hope; today I declare that I will restore to you double. 13 For I have bent Judah as my bow; I have made Ephraim its arrow. I will stir up your sons, O Zion, against your sons, O Greece, and wield you like a warrior's sword. 14 Then the LORD will appear over them, and his arrow will go forth like lightning; the Lord GOD will sound the trumpet and will march forth in the whirlwinds of the south. 15 The LORD of hosts will protect them, and they shall devour, and tread down the sling stones, and they shall drink and roar as if drunk with wine, and be full like a bowl, drenched like the corners of the altar. 16 On that day the LORD their God will save them, as the flock of his people; for like the jewels of a crown they shall shine on his land. 17 For how great is his goodness, and how great his beauty! Grain shall make the young men flourish, and new wine the young women.

What group of people is spoken of in these verses? We will now show two ways we know these verses are referring to Jesus helping the church.

    1. The blood of the covenant and the waterless pit (v. 11)
    2. Freed prisoners being restored double (v.12)

The Blood of the Covenant and the Waterless Pit (v. 11)

We will start by using verse eleven of Zechariah 9:11-17 to show this passage is speaking of the church.

Zechariah 9:11
11 As for you also, because of the blood of my covenant with you, I will set your prisoners free from the waterless pit.

THE SAINTS ARE "CAUGHT UP" (RAPTURE)

We need to determine two things in this verse: what covenant is mentioned, and what is the waterless pit. We will start by examining the waterless pit as it will shed light on the question of the covenant.

The Waterless Pit
The waterless pit is a reference to a prison. Below are two places in the Bible that mention a waterless pit. The first reference tells of Jeremiah's imprisonment during the Babylonian siege of Jerusalem, and the second tells of Joseph's brothers throwing him into a pit before deciding if they should kill him.

Jeremiah 38:6
⁶ So they took Jeremiah and cast him into the cistern of Malchiah, the king's son, which was in the court of the guard, letting Jeremiah down by ropes. And there was no water in the cistern, but only mud, and Jeremiah sank in the mud.

Genesis 37:24
²⁴ And they took him and threw him into a pit. The pit was empty; there was no water in it.

In both instances a pit, like a well with no water in it, is used as a prison to hold someone. So, a waterless pit is a prison but the word "pit" has another meaning given to it in the Bible. It has to do with death. Examples of this are shown in the next two verses.

Psalm 30:1-3
I will extol you, O LORD, for you have drawn me up and have not let my foes rejoice over me. ² O LORD my God, I cried to you for help, and you have healed me. ³ O LORD, you have brought up my soul from Sheol; you restored me to life from among those who go down to the pit.

Psalm 49:7-9
7 Truly no man can ransom another, or give to God the price of his life, 8 for the ransom of their life is costly and can never suffice, 9 that he should live on forever and never see the pit.

In both verses "the pit" is a reference to death. So, a waterless pit is a reference to a prison and "pit" has a second meaning of "death". We can see that freeing prisoners from the waterless pit could be interpreted as freeing them from death. Setting the prisoners free from the waterless pit in this case would be the resurrection. We will see this interpretation fits with the blood of the covenant.

The Blood of the Covenant

When we are told about the blood of the covenant, what covenant are we talking about? The Bible is divided into two covenants. The word "testament" literally means covenant. Both of these covenants were inaugurated with blood. Here is the blood of the Old Testament (covenant).

Exodus 24:8
8 And Moses took the blood and threw it on the people and said, "Behold the blood of the covenant that the LORD has made with you in accordance with all these words."

Here is the blood of the New Testament (covenant).

Matthew 26:27-28
27 And he took a cup, and when he had given thanks he gave it to them, saying, "Drink of it, all of you, 28 for this is my blood of the covenant, which is poured out for many for the forgiveness of sins.

We are told that the prisoners will be freed from the waterless pit due to the blood of the speaker's covenant. We need to find which covenant this action aligns with. Below is a section of scripture which compares both covenants.

THE SAINTS ARE "CAUGHT UP" (RAPTURE)

Hebrews 9:14-15
14 how much more will the blood of Christ, who through the eternal Spirit offered himself without blemish to God, purify our conscience from dead works to serve the living God. 15 Therefore <u>he is the mediator of a new covenant, so that those who are called may receive the promised eternal inheritance</u>, since a death has occurred that redeems them from the transgressions committed under the first covenant.

We see above that the blood of the new covenant allows the church to receive their eternal inheritance. We briefly covered the church's inheritance earlier in this book, but as a reminder the church receives this inheritance at the resurrection of the dead as shown below.

1 Corinthians 15:50-52
50 I tell you this, brothers: <u>flesh and blood cannot inherit the kingdom of God</u>, nor does the perishable inherit the imperishable. 51 Behold! I tell you a mystery. We shall not all sleep, but we shall all be changed, 52 in a moment, in the twinkling of an eye, at the last trumpet. For the trumpet will sound, and <u>the dead will be raised imperishable</u>, and we shall be changed.

If setting the prisoners free from the waterless pit is the raising of the dead, this would align with the blood of the new covenant. We have found the meaning of the blood of the covenant setting the prisoners free from the waterless pit. As further proof Zechariah 9 is speaking of the blood of the new covenant Hebrews 9 tells us directly what covenant Jesus is fulfilling at His second coming.

Hebrews 9:28
28 so Christ, having been offered once to bear the sins of many, will appear a second time, not to deal with sin but to save those who are eagerly waiting for him.

We can clearly see that at Jesus' second coming he is fulfilling the new covenant, saving the prisoners from the waterless pit. This proves Jesus is the one speaking in Zechariah 9 about the blood of the covenant. If you desire further proof I encourage you to study all of Hebrews chapter 9. Let's look again at our verse in Zechariah 9.

Zechariah 9:11
11 As for you also, because of the blood of my covenant with you, I will set your prisoners free from the waterless pit.

We now have interpreted what this verse is saying. Jesus tells us in this verse that because of His blood in the new covenant he will raise a group of people from the dead. We know this is the church being resurrected, because of Jesus' blood, as this is one of the most basic teachings of Christianity.

Freed Prisoners Being Restored Double (v.12)

Here is the second verse we will use to show Zechariah 9 is speaking of Jesus helping the church.

Zechariah 9:12
12 Return to your stronghold, O prisoners of hope; today I declare that I will restore to you double.

We already know that the prisoners are the church, so we will not prove this again. Can we now prove these prisoners receive a double restoration at the resurrection? We can find the answer in Isaiah 61 which also mentions a people set free from prison who receive a double restoration. These two things are underlined in the next passage.

Isaiah 61:1-7
The Spirit of the Lord GOD is upon me, because the LORD has anointed me to bring good news to the poor; he has sent me to bind up the brokenhearted, <u>to proclaim liberty to the captives, and the opening of the prison to those who are</u>

THE SAINTS ARE "CAUGHT UP" (RAPTURE)

bound; ² *to proclaim the year of the LORD's favor, and the day of vengeance of our God; to comfort all who mourn;* ³ *to grant to those who mourn in Zion— to give them a beautiful headdress instead of ashes, the oil of gladness instead of mourning, the garment of praise instead of a faint spirit; that they may be called oaks of righteousness, the planting of the LORD, that he may be glorified.* ⁴ *They shall build up the ancient ruins; they shall raise up the former devastations; they shall repair the ruined cities, the devastations of many generations.* ⁵ *Strangers shall stand and tend your flocks; foreigners shall be your plowmen and vinedressers;* ⁶ *but you shall be called the priests of the LORD; they shall speak of you as the ministers of our God; you shall eat the wealth of the nations, and in their glory you shall boast.* ⁷ <u>*Instead of your shame there shall be a double portion; instead of dishonor they shall rejoice in their lot; therefore in their land they shall possess a double portion;*</u> *they shall have everlasting joy.*

    I will start by mentioning that this is once again Jesus speaking. He quoted the first part of this verse, telling us he fulfilled it during his earthly ministry, in the New Testament (Luke 4:14-21). Just as in Zechariah 9:11-12, a people are mentioned who are set free from prison and given a double restoration. Unlike our last verse, much more is said about them here.
    Two clues in verse six tell us the identity of these people.

Isaiah 61:6
⁶ *but <u>you shall be called the priests of the LORD</u>; they shall speak of you as the ministers of our God; <u>you shall eat the wealth of the nations</u>, and in their glory you shall boast.*

    Let's examine the two underlined sections. First, we already know the priests of the Lord are the church. Recall that the church is referred to as being both kings and priests.
    For the "wealth of the nations" reference we only need to look one chapter back in Isaiah. This passage is one of many

other rapture references in the Old Testament we will not study in detail in this book. Our book focuses on the most detailed passages.

Isaiah 60:1-5
Arise, shine, for your light has come, and the glory of the LORD has risen upon you. ² For behold, darkness shall cover the earth, and thick darkness the peoples; but the LORD will arise upon you, and his glory will be seen upon you. ³ And nations shall come to your light, and kings to the brightness of your rising. ⁴ Lift up your eyes all around, and see; they all gather together, they come to you; your sons shall come from afar, and your daughters shall be carried on the hip. ⁵ Then you shall see and be radiant; your heart shall thrill and exult, because the abundance of the sea shall be turned to you, <u>the wealth of the nations shall come to you</u>.

We saw the rapture presented similarly in Joel 2:1-2.

Joel 2:1-2 (KJV)
Blow ye the trumpet in Zion, and sound an alarm in my holy mountain: let all the inhabitants of the land tremble: for the day of the LORD cometh, for it is nigh at hand; ² A day of darkness and of gloominess, a day of clouds and of thick darkness, as the morning spread upon the mountains: a great people and a strong; there hath not been ever the like, neither shall be any more after it, even to the years of many generations.

Both sections of scripture present a similar picture. Here are two similarities.
 1. Darkness is covering the earth.
 2. A light appears upon a people.

We have already proven the people in Joel 2:1-2 are the church. Because of the similarities between these two verses we can know that Isaiah 60:1-5 is speaking of the church as

THE SAINTS ARE "CAUGHT UP" (RAPTURE)

well. Because of this we know the people who receive the wealth of the nations in Isaiah 60:5 are the church. Let's now go back to Isaiah 61.

> Isaiah 61:1-7
> *The Spirit of the Lord G*OD *is upon me, because the L*ORD *has anointed me to bring good news to the poor; he has sent me to bind up the brokenhearted,* <u>*to proclaim liberty to the captives, and the opening of the prison to those who are bound;*</u> *² to proclaim the year of the L*ORD*'s favor, and the day of vengeance of our God; to comfort all who mourn; ³ to grant to those who mourn in Zion— to give them a beautiful headdress instead of ashes, the oil of gladness instead of mourning, the garment of praise instead of a faint spirit; that they may be called oaks of righteousness, the planting of the L*ORD*, that he may be glorified. ⁴ They shall build up the ancient ruins; they shall raise up the former devastations; they shall repair the ruined cities, the devastations of many generations. ⁵ Strangers shall stand and tend your flocks; foreigners shall be your plowmen and vinedressers; ⁶ but you shall be called the priests of the L*ORD*; they shall speak of you as the ministers of our God; you shall eat the wealth of the nations, and in their glory you shall boast.⁷* <u>*Instead of your shame there shall be a double portion; instead of dishonor they shall rejoice in their lot; therefore in their land they shall possess a double portion;*</u> *they shall have everlasting joy.*

We have shown from verse 6 above that the ones who are the priests of the Lord and receive the wealth of the nations are the church, so we know this entire section of scripture is referencing the church. Therefore, the church are the ones who are set free from prison and given a double portion in both Isaiah 61:1-7 and Zechariah 9:12.

Zechariah 9:12
¹² Return to your stronghold, O prisoners of hope; today I declare that I will restore to you double.

THE UNKNOWN RAPTURE SCRIPTURES

Putting Everything Together

We have shown Zechariah 9:11-17 is speaking of the church in two separate ways. We have also clearly shown this section of scripture is speaking of a resurrection through our study of the prisoners set free from the waterless pit who receive a double restoration. This means the events of these verses obviously occur at the time of the church's resurrection. Finally, we can tie this resurrection to the rapture through verse 14.

Zechariah 9:14
14 <u>Then the LORD will appear over them</u>, and his arrow will go forth like lightning; the Lord GOD will sound the trumpet and will march forth in the whirlwinds of the south.

We see Jesus will appear over the church at the time of the resurrection. The fact that Jesus appears in the air as the church is resurrected clearly shows this event is the rapture. As another confirmation we even see the trumpet blown in the verse above.

Let's review what we have discovered:
1. We know from previous chapters that the church is on the ground at the time of the resurrection. We also know this resurrection is described in our purposed rapture location.
2. From Zechariah 9:9-17 we know Jesus appears in the sky after this resurrection.
3. By proving the church joins Jesus in the sky after the resurrection we can prove our purposed rapture location is indeed the rapture.

As you can see only one step remains. We will examine a verse that mentions the church in the clouds at a later point on the day of the Lord. This will show the church does return to the clouds to meet Jesus in the air. First, here is our purposed rapture location once again.

THE SAINTS ARE "CAUGHT UP" (RAPTURE)

Revelation 14:14-16
14 Then I looked, and behold<u>, a white cloud, and seated on the cloud one like a son of man</u>, with a golden crown on his head, and a sharp sickle in his hand. 15 And another angel came out of the temple, calling with a loud voice to him who sat on the cloud, "Put in your sickle, and reap, for the hour to reap has come, for the harvest of the earth is fully ripe." 16 So he who sat on the cloud swung his sickle across the earth, and the earth was reaped.

In this verse we see the "one like a son of man" (the church) coming on the clouds prior to receiving their resurrected bodies. We will now examine another verse which will show the "one like a son of man" coming on the clouds of heaven "after" the resurrection. After we show this, we will be certain the church must return to the clouds after the resurrection to meet Jesus in the air.

Daniel 7:9-14
9 "As I looked, thrones were placed, and the Ancient of Days took his seat; his clothing was white as snow, and the hair of his head like pure wool; his throne was fiery flames; its wheels were burning fire. 10 A stream of fire issued and came out from before him; a thousand thousands served him, and ten thousand times ten thousand stood before him; the court sat in judgment, and the books were opened. 11 "I looked then because of the sound of the great words that the horn was speaking. And as I looked, the beast was killed, and its body destroyed and given over to be burned with fire. 12 As for the rest of the beasts, their dominion was taken away, but their lives were prolonged for a season and a time. 13 "I saw in the night visions, and behold, <u>with the clouds of heaven there came one like a son of man</u>, and he came to the Ancient of Days and was presented before him. 14 And to him was given dominion and glory and a kingdom, that all peoples, nations, and languages should serve him; his dominion is an everlasting

dominion, which shall not pass away, and his kingdom one that shall not be destroyed.

Here we see the same "one like a son of man", mentioned in our rapture defining scripture in Revelation. However, this section of scripture occurs AFTER the battle of Armageddon and AFTER Jesus (The Ancient of Days) has begun his rule on the earth. The "one like a son of man" (the church) is coming on the clouds of heaven meaning they returned to the clouds after their resurrection.

We have proven the following two things about our purposed rapture location in Revelation in this section"
1. Jesus appears in the sky after the church is resurrected.
2. The church returns to the clouds after the resurrection.

Through this we know the church meets Jesus in the air after the resurrection in our purposed rapture location.

Our purposed rapture location has passed its final test and has been confirmed to be the raptures location in Revelation.

11

Why the Rapture's Location has been Unknown

We have now seen proof of where the rapture is in Revelation. We studied the two most accepted verses relating to the rapture and determined these rapture defining scriptures occur in Revelation 14:14-16. We studied each section of this verse in detail to confirm this was the raptures location.

During our study we found additional places in the Bible that also spoke of the rapture. Below are six locations in the Bible we proved were speaking of the rapture. These are not used in current mainline rapture theories. These are the unknown rapture scriptures which our study has revealed.

Zechariah 3:8-10
⁸ Hear now, O Joshua the high priest, you and your friends who sit before you, for they are men who are a sign: behold, I will bring my servant the Branch. ⁹ For behold, on the stone that I have set before Joshua, on a single stone with seven eyes, I will engrave its inscription, declares the LORD of hosts,

and I will remove the iniquity of this land in a single day. ¹⁰ *In that day, declares the LORD of hosts, every one of you will invite his neighbor to come under his vine and under his fig tree."*

Ezekiel 37:1-14
The hand of the LORD was upon me, and he brought me out in the Spirit of the LORD and set me down in the middle of the valley; it was full of bones. ² *And he led me around among them, and behold, there were very many on the surface of the valley, and behold, they were very dry.* ³ *And he said to me, "Son of man, can these bones live?" And I answered, "O Lord GOD, you know."* ⁴ *Then he said to me, "Prophesy over these bones, and say to them, O dry bones, hear the word of the LORD.* ⁵ *Thus says the Lord GOD to these bones: Behold, I will cause breath to enter you, and you shall live.* ⁶ *And I will lay sinews upon you, and will cause flesh to come upon you, and cover you with skin, and put breath in you, and you shall live, and you shall know that I am the LORD."* ⁷ *So I prophesied as I was commanded. And as I prophesied, there was a sound, and behold, a rattling, and the bones came together, bone to its bone.* ⁸ *And I looked, and behold, there were sinews on them, and flesh had come upon them, and skin had covered them. But there was no breath in them.* ⁹ *Then he said to me, "Prophesy to the breath; prophesy, son of man, and say to the breath, Thus says the Lord GOD: Come from the four winds, O breath, and breathe on these slain, that they may live."* ¹⁰ *So I prophesied as he commanded me, and the breath came into them, and they lived and stood on their feet, an exceedingly great army.* ¹¹ *Then he said to me, "Son of man, these bones are the whole house of Israel. Behold, they say, 'Our bones are dried up, and our hope is lost; we are indeed cut off.'* ¹² *Therefore prophesy, and say to them, Thus says the Lord GOD: Behold, I will open your graves and raise you from your graves, O my people. And I will bring you into the land of Israel.* ¹³ *And you shall know that I am the LORD, when I open your graves, and raise you from your graves, O my people.*

THE UNKNOWN RAPTURE

¹⁴ And I will put my Spirit within you, and you shall live, and I will place you in your own land. Then you shall know that I am the LORD; I have spoken, and I will do it, declares the LORD."

Joel 2:1-2 (KJV)
Blow ye the trumpet in Zion, and sound an alarm in my holy mountain: let all the inhabitants of the land tremble: for the day of the LORD cometh, for it is nigh at hand; ² A day of darkness and of gloominess, a day of clouds and of thick darkness, as the morning spread upon the mountains: a great people and a strong; there hath not been ever the like, neither shall be any more after it, even to the years of many generations.

Isaiah 18:3
³ All you inhabitants of the world, you who dwell on the earth, when a signal is raised on the mountains, look! When a trumpet is blown, hear!

Isaiah 13:1-6
The oracle concerning Babylon which Isaiah the son of Amoz saw. ² On a bare hill raise a signal; cry aloud to them; wave the hand for them to enter the gates of the nobles. ³ I myself have commanded my consecrated ones, and have summoned my mighty men to execute my anger, my proudly exulting ones. ⁴ The sound of a tumult is on the mountains as of a great multitude! The sound of an uproar of kingdoms, of nations gathering together! The LORD of hosts is mustering a host for battle. ⁵ They come from a distant land, from the end of the heavens, the LORD and the weapons of his indignation, to destroy the whole land. ⁶ Wail, for the day of the LORD is near; as destruction from the Almighty it will come!

Zechariah 9:11-17
¹¹ As for you also, because of the blood of my covenant with you, I will set your prisoners free from the waterless pit.

¹² Return to your stronghold, O prisoners of hope; today I declare that I will restore to you double. ¹³ For I have bent Judah as my bow; I have made Ephraim its arrow. I will stir up your sons, O Zion, against your sons, O Greece, and wield you like a warrior's sword. ¹⁴ Then the LORD will appear over them, and his arrow will go forth like lightning; the Lord GOD will sound the trumpet and will march forth in the whirlwinds of the south. ¹⁵ The LORD of hosts will protect them, and they shall devour, and tread down the sling stones, and they shall drink and roar as if drunk with wine, and be full like a bowl, drenched like the corners of the altar. ¹⁶ On that day the LORD their God will save them, as the flock of his people; for like the jewels of a crown they shall shine on his land. ¹⁷ For how great is his goodness, and how great his beauty! Grain shall make the young men flourish, and new wine the young women.

In addition to these verses, we uncovered the name the Bible gives to the day of the rapture, which is the day of the Lord. We specifically studied the six sections of scripture above, but did not investigate most of the verses below, which also mention the day of the Lord.

Isaiah 2:12, 13:6, 13:9
Jeremiah 46:10
Ezekiel 13:5, 30:3
Joel 1:15, 2:1, 2:11, 2:31, 3:14
Amos 5:18, 5:20
Obadiah 1:15
Zephaniah 1:7, 1:14
Zechariah 14:1
Malachi 4:5
Acts 2:20
1 Corinthians 5:5
2 Corinthians 1:14
1 Thessalonians 5:2
2 Peter 3:10
Revelation 16:14

THE UNKNOWN RAPTURE

This list mentions many other places we could search for additional rapture details, including over twenty locations from the Old Testament alone. In addition to these, there are many more verses which speak of this day without specifically mentioning it by name. We found one of these in Isaiah 60. We have barely scratched the surface in understanding the day of the Lord. What we have done is prove the exact location of the rapture in Revelation and uncovered many details of the event.

As you can see, there is no shortage of information about the rapture of the church within the Bible. So why, to the best of my knowledge, have most of these verses, including almost every verse listed here from the Old Testament, never been included in any modern mainline study of the rapture?

The sad answer is these verses did not fit the theories theologians were trying to prove. Theologians were searching for verses which fit the theory rather than a theory that fit the verses. They should have investigated all scriptures relating to the rapture and continuously changed their understanding until the issue was settled. Instead, many chose to ignore verses which contradicted their original theory, telling themselves those verses were likely different events. So much was ignored to keep the theories valid that fewer than five sections of scripture were believed to relate to the rapture in many instances.

I want to give some examples of the contradictions which have been ignored, even within the remaining few scriptures scholars believe to be speaking of the rapture. I will start with a simple one to help us understand the type of contradiction to which I am referring, and will then show a large one which invalidates an entire rapture theory.

Let's begin in Matthew 24, which contains many details relating to time near the rapture. It is important that all these details align if we are to have a true interpretation. When these details do not align it creates confusion. As an example of two details of this chapter which are often given non-aligning interpretations, take the following two passages.

Matthew 24:26-27
26 So, if they say to you, 'Look, he is in the wilderness,' do not go out. If they say, 'Look, he is in the inner rooms,' do not believe it. 27 For as the lightning comes from the east and shines as far as the west, so will be the coming of the Son of Man.

Matthew 24:40-41
40 Then two men will be in the field; one will be taken and one left. 41 Two women will be grinding at the mill; one will be taken and one left.

Some interpret the second passage to be a place where Christians suddenly disappear, leaving those remaining wondering what has happened. However, this completely ignores the first passage which tells us all the world will see the return of Jesus. It will be no mystery what has happened when Jesus returns. This example shows how important it is to not ignore any verses in our interpretations. With that said, let's look at the most ignored verse in all of Matthew 24, underlined below.

Matthew 24:26-31
26 So, if they say to you, 'Look, he is in the wilderness,' do not go out. If they say, 'Look, he is in the inner rooms,' do not believe it. 27 For as the lightning comes from the east and shines as far as the west, so will be the coming of the Son of Man. <u>28 Wherever the corpse is, there the vultures will gather.</u> 29 "Immediately after the tribulation of those days the sun will be darkened, and the moon will not give its light, and the stars will fall from heaven, and the powers of the heavens will be shaken. 30 Then will appear in heaven the sign of the Son of Man, and then all the tribes of the earth will mourn, and they will see the Son of Man coming on the clouds of heaven with power and great glory. 31 And he will send out his angels with a

loud trumpet call, and they will gather his elect from the four winds, from one end of heaven to the other.

At first glance the underlined verse appears to not even belong in this passage or have anything to do with the rapture. That is exactly how it has been treated by many scholars. However, we will see that ignoring this verse caused the rapture to be misinterpreted to the point that no one knew where to find it in the book of Revelation. To interpret this verse let's look in the book of Luke where this phrase also appears.

Luke 17:34-37
34 I tell you, in that night there will be two in one bed. One will be taken and the other left. 35 There will be two women grinding together. One will be taken and the other left." 37 And they said to him, "Where, Lord?" He said to them, "<u>Where the corpse is, there the vultures will gather.</u>"

We will investigate what this phrase means from the book of Luke, since the book of Matthew does not supply any obvious surrounding details. I would first like to show that both chapters are speaking of the same event. I have shown in the table on the next page where everything mentioned in Luke 17:22-47 is found in Matthew 24. These verses are not chronological for Matthew 24 but are meant to show these two chapters are speaking of the same thing. Take a minute to examine this table before moving on.

By examining the verses of these chapters side by side it is easy to see they are speaking of the same event. We will now go through Luke 17:22-37 to understand the context of the phrase "Where the corpse is, there the vultures will gather".

We start out with Jesus telling His disciples that the whole world will see the Son of Man at His coming.

THE UNKNOWN RAPTURE SCRIPTURES

	Matthew 24	Luke 17
The coming of Jesus will be seen worldwide.	26 So, if they say to you, 'Look, he is in the wilderness,' do not go out. If they say, 'Look, he is in the inner rooms,' do not believe it. 27 For as the lightning comes from the east and shines as far as the west, so will be the coming of the Son of Man.	22 And he said to the disciples, "The days are coming when you will desire to see one of the days of the Son of Man, and you will not see it. 23 And they will say to you, 'Look, there!' or 'Look, here!' Do not go out or follow them. 24 For as the lightning flashes and lights up the sky from one side to the other, so will the Son of Man be in his day. 25 But first he must suffer many things and be rejected by this generation.
On the day of Jesus' return the believers will be saved and the unbelievers destroyed.	37 For as were the days of Noah, so will be the coming of the Son of Man. 38 For as in those days before the flood they were eating and drinking, marrying and giving in marriage, until the day when Noah entered the ark, 39 and they were unaware until the flood came and swept them all away, so will be the coming of the Son of Man.	26 Just as it was in the days of Noah, so will it be in the days of the Son of Man. 27 They were eating and drinking and marrying and being given in marriage, until the day when Noah entered the ark, and the flood came and destroyed them all. 28 Likewise, just as it was in the days of Lot—they were eating and drinking, buying and selling, planting and building, 29 but on the day when Lot went out from Sodom, fire and sulfur rained from heaven and destroyed them all— 30 so will it be on the day when the Son of Man is revealed.
Those taken and those left	40 Then two men will be in the field; one will be taken and one left. 41 Two women will be grinding at the mill; one will be taken and one left.	31 On that day, let the one who is on the housetop, with his goods in the house, not come down to take them away, and likewise let the one who is in the field not turn back. 32 Remember Lot's wife. 33 Whoever seeks to preserve his life will lose it, but whoever loses his life will keep it. 34 I tell you, in that night there will be two in one bed. One will be taken and the other left. 35 There will be two women grinding together. One will be taken and the other left."
The vulture reference	28 Wherever the corpse is, there the vultures will gather.	." 37 And they said to him, "Where, Lord?" He said to them, "Where the corpse is, there the vultures will gather."

THE UNKNOWN RAPTURE

Luke 17:22-25
22 And he said to the disciples, "The days are coming when you will desire to see one of the days of the Son of Man, and you will not see it. 23 And they will say to you, 'Look, there!' or 'Look, here!' Do not go out or follow them. 24 For as the lightning flashes and lights up the sky from one side to the other, so will the Son of Man be in his day. 25 But first he must suffer many things and be rejected by this generation.

Next, we are given two examples of what it will be like on the day the Son of Man is revealed.

Luke 17:26-30
26 Just as it was in the days of Noah, so will it be in the days of the Son of Man. 27 They were eating and drinking and marrying and being given in marriage, until the day when Noah entered the ark, and the flood came and destroyed them all. 28 Likewise, just as it was in the days of Lot—they were eating and drinking, buying and selling, planting and building, 29 but on the day when Lot went out from Sodom, fire and sulfur rained from heaven and destroyed them all— 30 <u>so will it be on the day when the Son of Man is revealed.</u>

We know that these two examples are describing the day of Jesus' return because we are told exactly that in the underlined section of the passage above. Both examples draw a contrast between believers and unbelievers. In the first example Noah is saved while the world is destroyed, and in the second example Lot is saved while Sodom is destroyed. Since these examples tell us what it will be like on the day where Jesus is revealed worldwide, we can make some conclusions.

On the day Jesus is revealed worldwide:
1. The unbelievers will be destroyed.
2. The believers will be saved.

THE UNKNOWN RAPTURE SCRIPTURES

With the message of these two examples in mind let's continue reading.

Luke 17:31-37
31 On that day, let the one who is on the housetop, with his goods in the house, not come down to take them away, and likewise let the one who is in the field not turn back. 32 Remember Lot's wife. 33 Whoever seeks to preserve his life will lose it, but whoever loses his life will keep it. 34 I tell you, in that night there will be two in one bed. One will be taken and the other left. 35 There will be two women grinding together. One will be taken and the other left." 37 And they said to him, "Where, Lord?" He said to them, <u>"Where the corpse is, there the vultures will gather."</u>

We are told of two groups of people in these verses. One group will be taken and the other left. It has always been assumed that the Christians are taken, but when his disciples asked him where those who were taken were to be brought, Jesus replied, <u>*"Where the corpse is, there the vultures will gather."*</u>

We can now interpret this phrase. The place described by the phrase *"Where the corpse is, there the vultures will gather."* is the location the people who are "taken" are brought in the verse *"One will be taken and the other left."*.

This does not sound like somewhere the church wants to be brought! Is it the church who are really taken here? Jesus told a parable describing this event which will give us our answer. This is another verse relating to the rapture which is ignored in current theories. We will look at both this parable and Jesus' interpretation of this parable to determine who is taken.

Matthew 13:24-30
24 Jesus told them another parable: 'The kingdom of heaven is like a man who sowed good seed in his field. 25 But while everyone was sleeping, his enemy came and sowed weeds

among the wheat, and went away. 26 When the wheat sprouted and formed heads, then the weeds also appeared. 27 "The owner's servants came to him and said, 'Sir, didn't you sow good seed in your field? Where then did the weeds come from?' 28 " 'An enemy did this,' he replied. "The servants asked him, 'Do you want us to go and pull them up?' 29 "'No,' he answered, 'because while you are pulling the weeds, you may root up the wheat with them. 30 Let both grow together until the harvest. At that time I will tell the harvesters: First collect the weeds and tie them in bundles to be burned; then gather the wheat and bring it into my barn.' "

Jesus explained this parable a few verses further down.

Matthew 13:36-43
36 Then he left the crowd and went into the house. His disciples came to him and said, "Explain to us the parable of the weeds in the field. "37 He answered, "The one who sowed the good seed is the Son of Man. 38 The field is the world, and the good seed stands for the sons of the kingdom. The weeds are the sons of the evil one, 39 and the enemy who sows them is the devil. The harvest is the end of the age, and the harvesters are angels. 40 "As the weeds are pulled up and burned in the fire, so it will be at the end of the age. 41 The Son of Man will send out his angels, and they will weed out of his kingdom everything that causes sin and all who do evil. 42 They will throw them into the fiery furnace, where there will be weeping and gnashing of teeth. 43 Then the righteous will shine like the sun in the kingdom of their Father. He who has ears, let him hear.

    To help make this easier to understand I have made a table so we can view the parable and interpretation side by side. You can view this table on the next page.

THE UNKNOWN RAPTURE SCRIPTURES

Matthew 13:24-30 (parable)	Matthew 13:36-43 (interpretation)
24 Jesus told them another parable: "The kingdom of heaven is like a man who sowed	36 Then he left the crowd and went into the house. His disciples came to him and said, "Explain to us the parable of the weeds in the field." 37 He answered, "The one who sowed the good seed is the Son of Man.
good seed in his field.	38 The field is the world, and the good seed stands for the sons of the kingdom.
25 But while everyone was sleeping, his enemy came and sowed weeds among the wheat, and went away.	The weeds are the sons of the evil one, 39 and the enemy who sows them is the devil.
26 When the wheat sprouted and formed heads, then the weeds also appeared. 27 "The owner's servants came to him him and said, 'Sir, didn't you sow good seed in your field? Where then did the weeds come from?' 28 "'An enemy did this,' he replied. 'The servants asked him, 'Do you want us to go and pull them up?' 29 " 'No,' he answered, 'because while you are pulling the weeds, you may root up the wheat with them. 30 Let both grow together until the harvest.	The harvest is the end of the age, and the harvesters are angels.
At that time I will tell the harvesters: First collect the weeds and tie them in bundles to be burned; then gather the wheat and bring it into my barn.' "	40 "As the weeds are pulled up and burned in the fire, so it will be at the end of the age. 41 The Son of Man will send out his angels, and they will weed out of his kingdom everything that causes sin and all who do evil. 42 They will throw them into the fiery furnace, where there will be weeping and gnashing of teeth. 43 Then the righteous will shine like the sun in the kingdom of their Father. He who has ears, let him hear.

THE UNKNOWN RAPTURE

This parable helps define who is taken when one is taken, and one is left. The "sons of the evil one" are taken <u>first</u>. The last comparison in the table makes this plain. So, when one is taken, and one is left, it is actually the nonbelievers who are taken. Matthew 13:39b (shown in the third comparison in the table) makes clear this event happens on the day of the rapture. I want to make clear that believers are raptured, as we have extensively studied. However, unbelievers will be taken in another event described by "one will be taken and another left". There is much more to this event, but it is once again beyond the scope of this book. As I stated before, I believe we are only covering about ten percent of the day of the Lord.

We have shown that ignoring the one underlined verse below has made huge changes to our understanding of this chapter.

Matthew 24:26-31
26 So, if they say to you, 'Look, he is in the wilderness,' do not go out. If they say, 'Look, he is in the inner rooms,' do not believe it. 27 For as the lightning comes from the east and shines as far as the west, so will be the coming of the Son of Man. <u>28 Wherever the corpse is, there the vultures will gather.</u> 29 "Immediately after the tribulation of those days the sun will be darkened, and the moon will not give its light, and the stars will fall from heaven, and the powers of the heavens will be shaken. 30 Then will appear in heaven the sign of the Son of Man, and then all the tribes of the earth will mourn, and they will see the Son of Man coming on the clouds of heaven with power and great glory. 31 And he will send out his angels with a loud trumpet call, and they will gather his elect from the four winds, from one end of heaven to the other.

Our new understanding of this verse completely invalidates the current pre-rapture theory. We have shown that the ones taken are not even the church! In fact, the ones taken are to be destroyed. Take a second to let that sink in.

THE UNKNOWN RAPTURE SCRIPTURES

The reason no one has been able to find the rapture in Revelation is almost entirely due to the misunderstanding of this fact. Do not ignore contradictions in your beliefs in scripture. Refine your beliefs through the word and be willing to change your views if your refinement fails. Most importantly, be willing to say "I don't know" instead of coming up with wild theories. Also, do not blindly follow other people's beliefs, but investigate everything yourself. I have done my best to give the scriptural basis for everything in this book, so anyone can easily check everything for themselves.

12

The Church of Revelation

The last issue I would like to discuss in this book is what everything we discovered means for the church? I do not want to leave anyone in fear of the coming events. I want to assure you that most of the other current teachings on Revelation are just as inaccurate as the teaching on the rapture.

The story of Revelation is the story of the events leading to the final victory of the church. The church has an exciting story, and does not, as has often been taught, just wait around suffering through all the end time events. The events in Revelation are all necessary steps making way for the fulfillment of the church's inheritance. In fact, the entire church will have a 3.5-year ministry which will closely resemble Jesus' earthly ministry within the timeframe of the book. We saw the church described as "one like a son of man" in this book and this is a due to a change which will occur in the church prior to Jesus' return. The implications of this and the knowledge of what the church will be doing during this timeframe of Revelation is incredible. The excitement does not end here. Going into the 1000-year Millennial reign, after the resurrection, the church will be established into the priesthood of Melchizedek, which Hebrews 6:20 tells us Jesus has entered as a forerunner on our behalf. Then into eternity. The Bible gives us some great clues to what the church will be doing, and it is not playing a harp on a cloud. This is just a small sampling of the many great things about the church recorded in Revelation.

In the description I just gave I likely went three or more books ahead of this one. Normally I would have waited to even mention some of these details, but I felt it was very important to not leave anyone believing that suffering was all that was awaiting the church during the end times. The church will accomplish everything Jesus has called it to accomplish. The church does not leave the world in failure only to have Jesus fix everything. Jesus loves us too much to see us fail the mission he has given us. The church will have its victory.

Many in the church do not see this victory. It has been widely taught that the influence of the church will greatly decline as the events of the rapture draw near. Persecution will certainly increase, but the church will not falter. In fact, the largest revival in the history of mankind will occur in the middle of Revelation. The church is too underdeveloped to accomplish God's future plan at present. The church must grow by leaps and bounds before they will be ready to accomplish God's purpose in the end times. The fact that the church is not ready may be one of the reasons we have been waiting for Jesus' return for over 2000 years. Consider the following passage.

2 Peter 3:8-13
8 But do not overlook this one fact, beloved, that with the Lord one day is as a thousand years, and a thousand years as one day. 9 The Lord is not slow to fulfill his promise as some count slowness, but is patient toward you, not wishing that any should perish, but that all should reach repentance. 10 But the day of the Lord will come like a thief, and then the heavens will pass away with a roar, and the heavenly bodies will be burned up and dissolved, and the earth and the works that are done on it will be exposed. 11 Since all these things are thus to

be dissolved, what sort of people ought you to be in lives of holiness and godliness, [12] waiting for and <u>hastening the coming of the day of God</u>, because of which the heavens will be set on fire and dissolved, and the heavenly bodies will melt as they burn! [13] But according to his promise we are waiting for new heavens and a new earth in which righteousness dwells.

Clearly the church can speed the coming of the day of the Lord as the underlined section above tells. The question asked through the centuries has been, "How long is Jesus going to wait?" The question we need to begin asking is, "How long are we going to make Jesus wait?"

The first step in making this change is to alter our thinking. It is not God's plan to have things get worse and worse until he finally removes us from the world. When we believe it is God's divine will that godliness must continually decline as the end times approach, it prevents us from taking action. Satan has used this false belief to trick much of the church into inactivity. Things are not going to get worse and worse for the church, but they will get better and better. The time of the book of Revelation will be the most successful period in the history of the church. This will all lead up to the final victory, the rapture on the day of the Lord.

www.ingramcontent.com/pod-product-compliance
Lightning Source LLC
Chambersburg PA
CBHW060837050426
42453CB00008B/729